POWER
in the
TONGUE

CAITLYN HUNTER

Tolsun Books
Flagstaff, Arizona

For Boosie, I miss you every day homie.

TABLE OF CONTENTS

*A bird does not sing because it has an answer,
it sings because it has a song.*—Maya Angelou

PROLOGUE

There's an age requirement to know their secrets. Knowing family history is grown folks' business. They'll leave you some breadcrumbs. They'll tell you the truth bombs mixed in with tall tales. By the time you're "grown enough," the stories have muddled together like cornbread mixed with pot likker held by fingertips. But there's always a lesson. There's always a purpose.

My favorite story is about a farm in Virginia. Grandpa would crack open an O'Doul's and pour himself a shot of vodka from a plastic bottle. He'd look over both sides of his shoulders and twist a large and broken knob from the mini television that sat on the dining room table. He'd wait for the "pop" of the knob and reach into the hollowed-out shell. From within the TV, he'd pull out a hidden piece of paper, examining it carefully as if he hadn't seen it a million times before. He'd chuckle. Just plain old beside himself, he'd put the paper face down between us. He'd wink as he'd slide the folded white piece of paper across the table. "You know," the story began, "we're sitting on a goldmine."

It was our little secret. Between him and me. He'd tell me about how we owned land. Land, on a farm with the largest uranium deposit in North America. Land—that with time and generations—

would make us as rich as the Carnegies themselves. All I had to do was *let my little light shine* and the rest would unfold just like that piece of paper.

It wasn't till I was an adult that I found out that this land and farm had another name: Plantation. I would eventually learn that we owned land on which we were owned. Land on which my great-great-grandfather Clem was lynched. Land my great-grandpa Jesse had to leave as sharecropping yielded nothing. Land on which my grandfather Archie was born and yet refused to name its traumatic legacy. None of that mattered.

He was proud of this land. Land which seeped with the blood and tears of our ancestors was and is and will forever be his. And because of this, Grandpa tried to control this narrative. Our "farm" was just a set piece against the backdrop of half-told stories about my ancestry. Stories whispered by word of mouth. Faces that would remain half-remembered by scattered photo albums in relatives' closets and dusty bookshelves. Someone needed to write it down. Someone needed to get these stories straight.

Our story, my story, isn't linear. Black stories shouldn't be reduced to one static format. They ebb and flow between rhythm and blues. We're all just making it up as we go along. We keep thriving and surviving, trying to keep up in time and pace. This much I've learned from the blueprints of my family's birdsong. The tune evolves as we continue to grow. The improvisation is complicated. To be Black and Woman are equally so. Perhaps I'm an unreliable narrator as my definitions of both continue to waver.

As a small child, my great-grandfather and I saw a magpie fly onto a bench while we took a walk in the park. The bird silently sat and stared at us. My great-grandfather bowed, and the bird returned the favor. They had a bond I did not understand. They both knew what it meant to fly.

When Great-Grandpa Jesse called him "brother," I knew then that the people in my family descended from magpies. We know when to swoop and fight and when to stop and contemplate our offerings. There is a twoness about us. Like the magpies, we symbolize luck and deception, and both are synonymous within our stories. There is always prosperity because in spite of it all, we've survived.

But allow me to get the lie straight. Let me drop some new knowledge on you of my lineage, like bars conscripted to dope beats. Allow me to tell you a tale that starts during a pandemic and with a dream...

There's a big house with an enormous dining room. And we're getting ready for dinner. And all seven of us—the four girls and three boys—are there. And this table is in the middle of the floor with a green tablecloth. Geneva is setting up the table and I'm cooking. And while I was making dinner, all three boys were gonna go out to the jacuzzi. But Joe was an adult. You see, he died when he was seven. And they were all gonna take a shower before jumping in the jacuzzi. It seemed like there was steam, rising from the shower that went up to the ceiling and went back down. Silas—I didn't see him naked—was in a towel. I yelled, "PUT SOME CLOTHES ON! I don't want you dragging water all through this dining room."

And then we have our dinner party. Your granddaddy is there, too. And he and Silas are just carrying on as ever. It's good to hear so much laughter. On the table are all my favorites of Mommy's cooking. Candied yams, fried chicken, pie, green beans—the works. Over dinner, Geneva and Marian are singing and Bea is just as jealous as always.

We take turns telling stories. Bragging about our kids, how our loved ones turned out. Telling tall tales like when we were children. Just good old catching up. All of them are there together again and me, the eldest, I'm just sitting at the end and I'm just as proud as ever…

"…It was a very pleasant dream."

My Aunt Bert leans back on the couch, her eyes still closed. "I'm 98 years old. I've lived a long life. But some days, I'm just so tired."

My aunt has outlived all her siblings. She's outlived friends. She's outlived two husbands. Sitting in her high rise on top of Hazelwood's hill—the very same building where my great-grandfather spent his last days—she sits and waits and goes through the motions.

I do my best to visit her. COVID-19 has changed the ways in which we interact and embrace. These visits require more precautions. Even still, day in and day out she wakes up, makes her bed, and puts on a little lipstick. Even today, she repeats the pattern. As she rubs a little rouge on her cheek, she turns and tells me, "I don't care if nobody sees me. I gotta look in the mirror *some time.*"

"I think," I tell her, "you got at least two more years in you."

"I dunno Cait, maybe."

I tell her I'm writing about her.

"About me?"

"Yes, you, Grandpa, Great-Grandpa, Mom, Wendell Scott, *everybody*. I want to tell our story."

She side-eyes me. "I think I'd like to read about that."

And so, I write.

Lesson One: Don't Forget Where You Came From

Fo Kuro Fun Ominira

There was a time long ago when African people could fly. They had magic. It was *old* magic where they could sing and turn into birds and soar high above the trees. But their enemies had nets. When they were captured and brought across the sea, their captors clipped their wings, stole their jewelry, and instead gave them shackles.

As they toiled in new lands under the blazing Southern sun, they kept their songs, but the language grew bitter and distorted on their tongues. Even so, they still had the same melody and rhythm lodged within their throats. As the cracks of whips lashed across their backs, they still stretched their arms to the skies, but the lift felt unfamiliar and so, they coped with newfound grounding.

One day, an enslaved woman laid an egg. From this egg, emerged a magpie. He was born with blue eyes and out of fear of losing him like she had with some many of her other children, the woman decided to never give the child a proper name.

Master loved his Magpie. Their eyes were the same cloudy-milk blue. The way Magpie's black feathers shone—like onyx radiating hints of purple in the sun—was mystical.

Every day, Master would open the cage, stroke his feathers, and wait for his bird to serenade him. And perched high on the windowsill, Magpie would sing for Master.

Yak yak yak, the bird would begin, *my Master's back.*
Today the tobacco will grow high.
Yak yak yak, there's talk of a Union attack.
Slavery's end is nigh.

"Slavery's end," chuckled Master. "Silly bird. The South will never go for it. We may be losing but the war is far from over." Master patted Magpie's head and locked the cage. Two days later, the war ended and Master's slaves were free.

Master couldn't lose his beloved bird. So, he and Magpie made a deal. "Stay with me, sweet Magpie. If you do, I'll release you from this cage and you can roam about my land as you see fit." Master offered his hand and Magpie shook it; after all, where would he go?

That night, while Magpie was sleeping, Master put a shackle with a long ball and chain on Magpie's foot. When Magpie awoke the next morning, he realized he was still out of the cage, but unable to shuffle any farther than the veranda.

Years passed and Magpie grew, but he still was awfully lonely. One day, Magpie sat on the front porch crying when a young girl walked by and offered him a tissue. "Pretty bird," she cooed, "why you crying?"

Yak yak yak, oh woe is me. Master has betrayed me.

Yak yak yak, I should be free, but now I'm chained in misery.

"Oh, poor darling," the girl gasped, and kissed Magpie on the forehead. "There, there, it's alright now." The girl reached into her apron and handed Magpie some cornbread wrapped in cloth. Magpie gobbled it up. It was the sweetest and softest bread he ever tasted. "My name's Nellie," the young girl said. She dusted herself off, and grabbed the basket of laundry, hoisting it on her hip. "Be seeing you!" With that, she walked away.

Magpie was in love, and he molted with the longing. With every wilting feather, the Master saw an opportunity growing. "Hey Magpie?" Master coyly asked. "I know I tricked you but hear me out. If I give you a plot of land and you promise to stay, I'll let you marry that girl."

Yak yak yak, I'll shake on that.
Yak yak yak, she makes me so happy.
Yak yak yak, I'll stay and work.
Yak yak yak, I'll be free with Nellie.

And with that, Magpie and Master shook hands and soon after, Magpie and Nellie were married.

But the land Master gave Magpie was rotten. Nothing grew, nothing lived. Magpie and Nellie now had children in a little shack high on the hill. Magpie and Nellie toiled and tilled dry plots of dirt where not even tobacco could be bothered to grow. Work got so hard that Nellie's brothers had to help, but even then, all they could reap was dying weeds and dust. When harvest time came, Master asked Magpie what he had to sell.

Yak yak yak, my crops I lack.
There's nothing here to sell.
Yak yak yak, we broke our backs.
But there's nothing here to till.

"Now, Magpie," Master said, shaking his head, "I expected better from you. I gave you a plot of land. Looks like you owe me more, and I'll just add it to your debt."

Magpie and Master shook hands, and Magpie went home to his wife and children.

Yak yak yak, that Master's a crook.
We'll die here if we stay.
Yak yak yak, there is no food.
I'll find work. I'll always find a way.

Nellie agreed and packed her husband a bag. She put some chicken, some cornbread, and some salt pork in a cloth and handed it to Magpie. She kissed him on the beak and wished him luck. Magpie kissed his family goodbye, lifted his arms, and flew.

He flew from town to town looking for work. First, a town outside Chatham, Virginia. Then, Maryland. Then, Pennsylvania. Each farm offered a little more money than the next, and whatever he earned, Magpie sent to Nellie and the children.

One day as he was flying around, a large cloud of black fog made him cough and blinded his eyes. A gust of cold wind stiffened his wings and before Magpie knew it, he hit a brick smokestack.

Magpie rubbed his eyes and saw a sign: STEEL MILL WORKERS

FOR HIRE. He followed the men towards the factory and stood in the soot-covered crowd. A man with a hard hat came out. "Alright fellas, we're looking for twenty men. Who here can work?"

All of the men raised their hands high in the air. Magpie did the same. One by one, people in the crowd were chosen. "One, two, three, four…" Magpie jumped a little higher.

"Five, six, seven, eight… No! Not you! How about the Italian over there?" Magpie spread his wings letting the air around him hoist him higher as the choosing went on.

"Seventeen, eighteen, nineteen… Hey You! The bird with the blue eyes." Magpie pointed to himself. "Yeah, guy. You! C'mon. You're hired."

As Magpie jumped down and shuffled his way through the crowd the foreman concluded, "Okay guys, that's it. Come back tomorrow to see if we'll need replacements."

The men in the crowd grumbled. The twenty selected made their way to the front. The men gave their names to the foreman and he gave them each a ticket.

Magpie looked at the ticket in his hand and took one last look at the sky. He didn't need to fly anymore. Up North, there was opportunity. Up North, he could be his own master. In Pittsburgh, Magpie decided he and his family would roost.

Retched of the Earth

You look visibly uncomfortable." Makai snaps another picture. I readjust my "Abolitionist" t-shirt to hide the grease stain left by fish bait. She positions me in front of the sign and takes another photo. It has been twenty years since I last stepped foot onto Sotterley. Twenty years since I've been to any plantation.

Sotterley sits on 94 acres of fields and trees nestled along the shorelines of the Chesapeake Bay. It is thought to be "a romantic emblem of the colonial past." In its heyday, Sotterley was considered the largest plantation in Maryland—both in acreage and wealth—as the plantation owned 41 enslaved Africans in the 18th century. It was former land of the Patuxent tribe. Colonial settlement and harsh treatment of the terrain forced the Indigenous population to relocate. Now the only remaining Tidewater plantation open to the public, it hosts weddings, private events, and family-friendly educational programs.

"How does it feel to be back here?" Makai asks as she continues to take photos of the farmhouse behind me. How do I even begin to answer her? I feel irritable. I feel frustrated. I feel vulnerable. I feel like that farm-girl child once again. I feel like I am going to vomit.

My finger pokes a hole in the dirt. Red and sepia clay cakes underneath my fingertip. The Earth is warm. Inviting for a seed. I drop one in, covering my hand with the soil, and say a prayer. "May you grow into greatness." I use my feet to measure the distance. One foot by one foot I count to the next unsuspecting mound of dirt I will impregnate. Another finger. Another prayer. This is the way. By the time I am done, Johnny has already planted three rows to my one. He smiles at me with buck teeth and wipes the dirt onto his pants. "Maybe you're not meant to be a farmer, Cait."

"Oh yeah? Well, what am I *supposed* to be then?"

"I dunno…" Johnny retorts. "Maybe my wife."

We laugh and I chase him through the plowed field throwing pebbles until one lands on his back. He says, "I have a surprise for you today. Let's go to our castle."

We grab our bikes and ride to the hill that sits between Johnny's house and mine. We scale the side of it that overlooks a small pond. We wrestle. We pretend we are Power Rangers trying to beat Zod and blast him back into space. We roll down the side of the hill letting the mud and grass stain our blue jeans. We lay on the banks of the pond or, as we called it, our moat, and Johnny points to it. There's a clear blob with little black specks inside. He grabs a stick and pokes it. The specks frantically move around, swirling, bobbing against the sides of the blob like a bowling ball into bumper lanes.

"What is that?" I ask, bending down to get a closer look.

"They look like tadpoles," Johnny replies, "I've seen 'em dozens of times with Dad at the other pond by our house."

"But, why are they in there?"

Johnny scratches his head and shrugs his shoulders. "I guess they're stuck. Maybe a witch put a curse on them, and they're trapped."

I squeeze Johnny's arm. "We must help them."

"Never fear!" Johnny exclaims. He takes his stick and pokes the blob with holes. Like a bursting balloon, the tadpoles rush out into the pond. We dance holding hands at the feat of conquering their gelatinous prison. We watch as the tadpoles squiggle and squirm on the shore, Johnny taking his stick to push the weaker ones into the safety of the water.

My mother worked a lot in my childhood. She was the Dean of Students at the local college. Johnny's parents, Don and Dee, were like my second parents and they often looked after me. His sisters Adele and Ashlee were the sisters I always wanted. His mother was Black like mine, with beautiful dark brown skin that always glowed and glistened with sweat in the sun. His father, I always believed, was half giant with the way he would tower over us, but Johnny assured me it was because he was Italian. But Johnny's skin was like my skin—the same caramel complexion that tanned red in the sun. His hair was like my hair—the same tough and coily texture that sponged up water when wet. Johnny was mine entirely.

Wherever Johnny went, so did I. Whatever I did, he wasn't too far behind. Through him, I had found a place where I belonged. He knew the lay of the farmland. He spoke the Earth's language. He knew the magic of life.

When Johnny got chicken pox, we laid together under sleeping bags in long johns in the living room by the wood stove. His mother taped oven mitts over his hands, and I would scratch the places he couldn't reach. I grabbed his pustule-riddled face and let him breathe into mine as he insisted that this was the cure, and I would never get sick. And when I left his house after our sleepover with no pox on my body, much to my mother's dismay, I knew his magic had worked.

That following spring, when the nanny goat Bambi reared her head preparing to charge, Johnny stood in front of me. In the split second before her head made contact, Sergeant, the German shepherd, dashed between our five-year-old bodies and ripped out the goat's throat. Johnny covered my eyes. His shirt, pants, and hands were still warm and sticky with the goat's blood as he took me to hide behind the barn. I don't remember the screams. I don't remember the warning. But I remember the dog whose heroism also threatened a farmer's livelihood and could be rendered dispensable. Johnny held my head in between his hands covering my ears as his father's gun fired and muffled the dying whimpers of Sergeant. His hands, his warm and chapped hands, had the ability to silence the world's chaos.

When we started school together, me wearing his older sister's yellow hand-me-down blouses, complete with matching yellow-brown plaid skirts, the penny loafers were his. He taught me, "Put a penny into the tip of the shoe and you'll have good luck all day." My mother met me at the bus stop after that first day of Catholic school with a McDonald's Happy Meal. I was convinced then that any pennies from Johnny's pockets could perform miracles.

Climbing trees and learning how to read their branches, riding my bike on dirt roads, whispering into eggs before they hatched, telling when fruit was ripe enough to pick from the stalk by squeezing—all were part of my upbringing with Johnny. To grow up on a farm was to learn the alchemy of nature, and Johnny was my teacher.

When my mother got a job at a college in Ohio, I remember the day I said goodbye to Johnny. He was crying uncontrollably. I wiped away his tears and promised that I would be back. "Nothing will change," I swore. "You'll see! I'll write to you all the time and come visit." He begged for me not to leave even though there was nothing I could do. We were to leave for Ohio, and I had no say. Three years passed between us. We wrote to each other once but with age, we both moved on.

Eventually, I moved back to the farm, but the magic had changed. The language became foreign. We were both now eleven, and while I started public school, Johnny remained in Catholic school. Even with living on the same farm, puberty created a new borderland where rows of Christmas trees between his home and mine outlined its perimeter.

To our surprise, we ended up going to high school together. Every morning we'd stand at the bus stop on Willow Road six feet apart with backs turned away from one another. We'd pretend to fixate on anything we could and wait until the bus could save us from this awkward silence.

After climbing aboard the bus, we went through our routines. Sit on opposite ends of the bus. Go to school and hang with friends. Attend opposite after-school activities. While Johnny played junior varsity basketball, I was making out with boys and letting them touch my budding breasts underneath the bleachers. When I cheered at football games and raised pompoms high in the air, Johnny would skateboard with some white boys in the school parking lot, his knees scraped, and his elbows bleeding onto pavement. On rare occasions we'd take the bus home together.

After we both stepped off the bus, the long legs he got from his daddy always carried him faster and further away from me. We'd split at the fork in the road and the day was done. If we passed by each other in the hallways in school, there'd be a nod or a wave, but that was that. After the bus stop and fork in the road, we'd go our separate ways.

In our third year of high school, we both had to take the same U.S. History class. Instead of teaching us about the Civil War, the school district's curriculum thought it best to send us to plantations on field trips.

I knew of plantations. Watching *Gone with the Wind* with my mother, the romanticized Tara was deeply ingrained as the model of life on a plantation. It was a place that was grandeur incarnate. It was a place that felt strong and felt safe. We'd laugh at Hattie Mc-Daniel's facial expressions. We'd swoon over Clark Gable's bravado. We'd mourn with Scarlett at the loss of her children as Vivian Leigh educated me on the ways of womanly charm and perseverance. But nothing is ever like the movies, is it?

Through the scattered trees our bus rumbled along the dirt road as spit balls and notes passed between bus seats. The large brick house with tall red chimneys and white painted columns and trim was the very pinnacle of the romantic South surrounded by rolling fields of grass and tobacco stalks. We pulled up to a white picket fence and a woman opened the front door of the house. "Hello," she waved, motioning us to come closer.

This wasn't like home. The smell felt stale and the air reeked of hay and salt. The ground beneath my feet felt hard as the gravel under my sandal was unforgiving. The woman brushed her blond hair out of her face and gathered the group close. "Welcome to Sotterley Plantation, home of the colonial South and romantic past." She gestured towards the large white house. "Here, we will start our tour with one of my favorite places, Sotterley Manor."

We walked up the wooden steps, the floorboards creaking under our feet, and into a grand parlor where a staircase with patterned banisters unfolded before us. I had never seen anything so extravagant. Each room had a theme, a color, a tribute to its white ownership through portraiture. The guide continued her stories, the origin of each room's design. "The drawing room," she told us, "is inspired by Greco-Roman design. The motifs in the woodwork as seen in the mantel have been here since the 18th century."

I imagined being in a grand salon with women in gold and green taffeta dresses. I imagined drinking tea and eating delicate cakes and cucumber sandwiches. I imagined tight ringlets of hair adorned with colorful bows and ribbons volumized by gossip between each strand and I among them, fanning myself in the warm, tepid air that wisped around me. The guide motioned to another room, disrupting my daydream.

Bored, I slipped away back out of the parlor. Classmates took pictures. Some of them laid in the grass or sat in the rocking chairs on the porch. The gardens beside the manor were reminiscent of a Grecian labyrinth. I slipped between topiaries, my fingers tracing the path towards the croquette field as if I was looking for my Minotaur, a monstrous foreboding.

In the clearing there was a sundial. A compass in the middle of it directed my fingers North towards the river. The farm seemed like any farm: a large white barn off in the distance, goats bleating and nearby hens clucking. I felt like Tara.

Then I heard some laughter. On the other side of the manor, Johnny and a few boys stood by a shed where they tousled each other around and played out in front. One of the other boys waved me over. He pointed to the shed behind him which, upon a closer look, I realized had a chimney. "That's where *your* people lived."

My people? I gave the boy a quizzical look.

He pointed inside. "Go see for yourself."

The building was tattered, about one sixteenth the size of the Manor. Inside the dismal brown wooden walls was one room, one bed, and a small wooden table. People? As in more than one had lived here? In the hearth, one small dusty cast iron pot sat in the middle.

There were no pictures, no Greco-Roman intricacies on the mantle. There was pain. A cold damp pain etched into the floor and walls. I shivered and exited the cabin.

"My people never lived here," I told the boy. "My people come from greatness."

He rolled his eyes and spat at the Earth. "Don't be a stupid nigger," he retorted. The other boys joined him in laughter, and they walked away.

I stared at that cabin. Its trauma echoed. Reverberated as much as the harshness of the hard *g*'s and hard *r* from the boy's words. This silent cacophony paralyzed me. A hand on my shoulder snapped me out of it. I turned, and it was Johnny.

"You don't owe *them* anything."

Before I could respond he walked away and rejoined the tour. On the bus ride home, all I could think about was that boy's words and Johnny's response. *My people. Them.* Johnny understood something that I could not. Even with growing up on the same farm with the same people, he knew that Sotterley meant something else. It was a place where we didn't belong. We were not them. We were "other." Sotterley was not Tara. I would never be Scarlett O'Hara, not to them, not to *anyone*.

The bus doors opened, and Johnny and I walked off. With perfect timing, like always, his legs carried him faster and further than I could keep up. With each step I thought of the ways I wanted to talk to him. Ask him what he meant. Tell him thank you. Just say something, anything. But before I could utter anything we came to the fork in the road. I watched him walk away, kicking up clouds of dirt and pebbles. He disappeared over the horizon. I remember standing there and staring, hoping that some curiosity, some gut intuition, would have made him stop. He never looked back.

"I can't believe you lived here." The car jumbles against the edges of worn-down potholes on the dirt like pinballs bouncing off archways. The canopy of pollen-covered trees shades us from the thick humid air. It has been two months since my last visit to Sotterley and Southern Maryland. It's been over a decade since I've been back to Flower of the Forest farm. As we continue to drive, there are newly constructed homes where there was once an unaltered strip of forest. Even still, the dirt and cobbled path leading to my childhood home remains unphased. "We're almost there," I tell my boyfriend, Nick.

Rows of apple trees on one side and Christmas trees on the other greet us at a looming fork in the road. Excitedly, I point to each plot of land.

"There's where I used to pick asparagus to eat on my way home from school. Ooh! And there's where we used to plant strawberries. And down there is the blueberry patch! That's where I learned to ride a bike and…"

And then I see it. Off in the clearing, the old farmhouse comes into view. The same red brick building with wraparound porch, the pond, and the barn behind it are still there. Nothing is gone. Nothing is different. Despite two decades of life gone by since I last stepped foot on Johnny's porch, the magic of this land remains. The farm, *our* farm, has been molded, time-casted into a capsule. The pockets of memories live on and take root.

We turn off the car and I walk up the stairs. In the sunroom Don, Johnny's father, sits reading his newspaper. His hair is now white, but his face and his long legs remain unchanged.

"Hi, Mr. Don!" I wave through the screen door. Baffled, he leans in close to get a better view of who is standing in front of him. Ms.

Dee leans over from the other side of the couch. She puts down her bowl of shucked green beans.

"Caitlyn?" In utter disbelief, she opens the door with arms opened wide for an embrace. The child she helped to raise stands in front of her now a woman. It didn't matter if Johnny never looked back. I had to find the magic on my own. This farm, this place, this town would forever be my home.

Lesson Two:
You Don't Always Get to Pick and Choose Your Battles

O Kan Wakọ

Once upon a time, there was a boy. And he was not no ordinary boy. Oh no. This boy could fix *anything*. Day after day he worked in his daddy's tool shed tinkering away on old appliances that no longer wanted to work, fixing toys that needed mending, and reconstructing old motors and engines that coughed and sputtered back to life. More than anything else, he dreamed about flying.

It was an ordinary day. As the sun rose and the cock crowed, the boy knew that work needed to be done. Daddy knocked on the door. "Wendell, my boy. Time's a wastin. Got a car in the shed that needs fixin. Gotta go to town. Be back in three days."

"Okay, Daddy," Wendell said, wiping the crust from his eye. "I'll get right on it."

Wendell put on his overalls and boots and went to the shed. He changed the tires. Took the old ones and made them into new soles for his boots. He tinkered with the engine. It whirred, chugging for breath. Wendell looked in the exhaust pipe and pulled out feathers. *Wonder how these got here,* he thought to himself, putting them in his back pocket. Wendell took out the seats and replaced the fabric with a soft ivory leather that felt like just-churned butter. By the time he washed and polished the silver car, it looked brand new.

"Pheeeeeeewiiiiiieeeeeee," Wendell whistled. "Now that's a *fine* beauty."

"I dunno," said a grisly voice. "But can she *fly?*"

A cat was sitting by the shed door licking its paw. Its tail forked right at the tip. The cat walked up to Wendell, sauntered over real nice like. But a cat's only nice when it wants something.

The voice rasp-purred again, "Can this beauty fly, faster, farther, than others?" The flick of the tips of the cat's split tail caught Wendell's eye. The cat wrapped its tail around Wendell's boot. He took a step back from the cat.

"Who are you, lil devil?" Wendell asked.

"You should know," smiled the cat. "You called me by name."

"I ain't call nobody! I'm just here mindin my own business."

"Oh, you should know better than to whistle unless you want *my* business."

The cat hunched over and got a bit bigger. It stood on its hind legs and its ears became little horns. "Tell you what; let's make a deal. I'm just starting out, you see. And I need to make some business if I want to keep my job. You race me with this car, and if you beat me, I'll grant you a wish."

"A wish," Wendell asked, "for anything I want?"

"Anything."

Wendell scratched his head. "And what do I have to give you in return?"

"Oh nothin," said the Lil Devil, "except your soul. But you ain't using it anyways."

The deal was too good to pass up. He shook the Devil's hand. "You got yoself a deal."

The Lil Devil smiled. "Meet me here tomorrow. After the cock crows three times." With a poof, Lil Devil disappeared.

Wendell finished his farm chores, ate some supper, and went to bed. Like always, he dreamed of flying.

In the night, Lil Devil snuck into the shed. He stuck magpie feathers into both exhaust pipes. He was goin to win this race, for sure.

Just like clockwork, the cock crowed. Wendell jumped up, put on his overalls, his boots, and raced to the barn. Lil Devil was there, just a-grinning as ever, standing next to his very own car, the same exact make and model as Wendell's. But this car was a candy apple red.

"Ready to race?"

"Sure as I'll ever be."

Wendell and Lil Devil got into their cars, and they fired up both engines. Lil Devil gave the signal.

"On your mark...get set...GO!"

The engines roared as the tires kicked up dust clouds in the air. Wendell and Lil Devil were neck and neck and then, all of a sudden, Wendell's car whirred. It coughed and sputtered, and died. Lil Devil sped past, leaving Wendell in his dust.

Wendell got out of the car, looked at the exhaust pipe, and pulled out feathers. The black and white feathers felt familiar in his hands. He put them in his back pocket with the others.

Lil Devil circled back and pulled up alongside Wendell. "A deal's a deal boy. Hand me over that soul."

"You sure are right," Wendell replied. He reached down to the bottom of his boot and ripped off the sole. "Here, as promised, Lil Devil, one sole."

Lil Devil's smile turned into a frown. "What is this?" He scowled. "I wanted your soul."

"Mhmm," Wendell replied. "And I got one more good one. How about another race? Double or nothin?"

Lil Devil needed a soul to take to his boss. "Okay," Lil Devil replied. "Double or nothin. But this time, no tricks! Meet me again tomorrow morning when the cock crows three times."

Wendell and Lil Devil shook hands and then—with a *poof*—Lil Devil disappeared. Wendell cleaned up the car, finished his farm chores, and ate some supper. During dinner, Wendell told Momma about his race.

"Sounds to me like Lil Devil played a trick on you," said Momma. "Before you go to bed, take this big mirror down to the shed and put it on the door. That'll teach him."

Wendell did as he was told and put the mirror on the shed door. He went to bed and dreamed of flying.

Just like the night before, Lil Devil tried to sneak into the shed. But this time, no matter how hard he tried, he couldn't get past the front door. He banged, and kicked, and cussed, but there was no budging. Instead, he went to the chicken coop to kill that rooster. He found a bird roosting and put his hands around its neck until it went limp. He was going to win this race, for sure.

Too bad Lil Devil was never a farmer. A good farmer knows the rooster never sleeps with the hens. Just like clockwork the cock crowed. Wendell jumped up, put on his overalls, his boots, and raced to the barn. Lil Devil was there standing next to his very own car, the same exact make and model as Wendell's, but this car was now as black as tar.

"Ready to race?"

"Sure as I'll ever be."

Wendell and Lil Devil got into their cars. They fired up both engines. Lil Devil gave the signal.

"On your mark…get set…GO!"

And they were off. Wendell and Lil Devil speeding neck and neck. But this time, Wendell reached into his pocket and threw the magpie feathers in Lil Devil's face. Lil Devil howled and snarled and veered off the road. Wendell kept driving, fast as four wheels would fly. He passed trees and rivers. He passed crossroads. Lil Devil tried to catch up, but he couldn't. Wendell kept going, kept him in the rearview the whole time.

Wendell would grow up to become the first Black NASCAR driver. He'd win more money than he could count. He'd win trophies. He'd fly further and faster than anyone because he learned quick that you always need to keep the devil in the rear-view.

AWOKEN

The drive between Maryland and Pittsburgh is my songbird journey. There are always reasons to fly Southward and return. The four-hour-long stretch of roads over mountains, through tunnels, past the occasional rest stop are circadian landmarks.

Birds, like me, have an internalized compass. They draw their information from the sun, the stars, and by sensing the earth's magnetic pull. During this flight, I try to drive at a safe speed. Never going more than five miles over the limit, I know all it takes is one speed trap to give due cause for a State Trooper to meet their quota. I see a cop parked on the side of the road, and I reduce my speed to 55. But then I see the lights flash in my rear-view.

Red.

Blue.

White.

Shit. What did I do now?

I hear the wailing whomps of the siren.

I pull over.

Okay. Deep Breaths.

I put my license and registration in my lap and keep my hands on the wheel. A man, short with a square torso and black hair, exits the car. With each step he takes towards me, I try to remember to breathe.

"Good afternoon," he starts. "You know why I pulled you over?"

Driving while Black? I think. Instead, I reply, "I'm sorry. No, sir. I don't. I didn't think I was speeding."

"Well, I was on the side of the road and about to pull out and you cut me off."

Wasn't he parked? "I'm sorry, sir. No, I must've not seen your signal. I've been driving for some time now as I'm heading home to school from visiting family."

*There. That should show him I'm not **that** kind of person.*

I'm the kind of person who "speaks good."

The kind of person who is the very model of Du Bois' talented 10th.

I am not his Negro.

He looks into my car, gives me a once over. "Hm. I see. License and registration." I hand him the stuff sitting on my lap and put my hands back on the wheel. Like most children with Black parents, I was taught about how to deal with police:

Yes, sir.

No, ma'am.

Hands at ten and two.

Don't give them a reason.

Show them that you matter.

Do what you must to make it home to your mother.

Stay woke.

Survive.

"Wait here, I'm going to check on your information."

He walks back to his car. I sit in silence. I know I've done nothing wrong, but even still, the panic sets in. You'll go a whole lifetime dealing with those who have sworn to protect you. There is a part of you that will always be fearful. There is always a part of you that wonders if you will make it home. Every time feels like the first time. Every time feels like that moment. The one you'll never forget…

Clouds of smoke whirl around us in the room, mixing with Nag Champa incense. We bathe in a vacuum of sweet herbal bliss. I take another hit of the blunt and pass it to my boyfriend, John. On TV, Manny Pacquiao slays another foe between the ropes with a right hook made of lead. "Why didn't your boy come in?" Don asks, swiping his dreads out of his face and looking at his watch. With each passing minute we were wearing out our welcome.

"I dunno," John replies. "His girl said she had a headache, so they stayed in the car. I guess we better go. It's been about 30 minutes."

We leave the apartment and stand outside. Cubby, Don's cousin, hunches over a grill pit. The aroma of searing chicken lacquered with sweet and tangy Mambo sauce hits me in the stomach. Children around us scream and run, playing a game of tag in the street.

Go-go drums clap and vibrate through the stereo. John and Don take turns b-boying. Flipping over one another, crip walking, and dabbing. I consider myself impressed that my white boy got moves. We hug goodbye, and Don tells me to "Take it easy." High off the fumes of the blunt, high off the warmth of Don and the setting sun's glow over the Anacostia skyline, we walk back to the car where Jamie and his girl Eve are napping in the front.

"Y'all have fun?" Jamie asks, readjusting his seat.

"Yeah," John replies. "They're good people."

Eve sleepily leans onto the side of the passenger window as Jamie puts the key into the ignition. We make it down the block. Before Jamie can turn on his blinker, there are flashing red and blue lights.

Three cop cars pull up to the front, back, and side of us. Six cops run toward us, guns drawn, flashes of black metal tapping on windows. They scream. "GET OUT OF THE CAR! GET OUT OF THE FUCKING CAR NOW!"

I am confused. *Is there some kind of mistake?*

The cops open our doors and grab my arm. The grasp squeezes tight as I feel my own pulse under the weight of a thumb.

"STAND HERE." I am on the wall pressed against concrete. I feel hands between my legs. Between my thighs. "WHERE ARE THE DRUGS, BITCH? WE KNOW YOU HAVE THEM."

I stand, helpless, and look for John. He is standing with Jamie and Eve on the other side of the car. The cops are asking them questions. Our eyes meet. My eyes plead for him to help me. He looks down.

"WHERE ARE THE DRUGS?" A white cop turns me around. As he sticks his hands down my dress and gropes my breasts, all I can do is fixate on his silvery white hair. I count the follicles. I stare at each strand and think about how the peppering of silver is so much like my mother's.

"Please," I ask him. "Please, I don't have anything."

"I KNOW YOU'RE LYING, BITCH," he tells me. He takes a deep breath. "WHERE IS THE DOPE?" He takes the black beret off my head. The beret my grandfather gave me and told me to always let my light shine. A flashlight shines in my face as the cop sticks his hands in my hair. He shakes my curls and bends me over to make sure something falls out.

He sits me on the curb of the sidewalk, and more officers put my hands behind my back. I am facing my friends. They are facing away. They ask Eve and Jamie if they can search the car, they give their permission. A Black cop goes directly to my side of the car and grabs my purse. He goes through my wallet and pulls out a card. He looks at the card, looks at me, and then walks over to the white cop to show him. On the back I see it is my college ID; the weathered black band of my meal swipe card seems to be my only ticket out of this mess.

The Black cop walks over to me and stands me up. He loosens my restraints and hands me my purse. "You know it's lucky we got to you when we did," he tells me. "The house you came out of is a trap house. A lot of bad drug deals come out of there." He smiles, as if this is to reassure me. Perhaps out of shock, I thank him, even though I don't know why.

The cops hand the keys back over to Jamie and they tell us that we're free to go. John and Jamie thank the cops and we get back into the car. The white cop tells them to "get home safe." We leave Minnesota Ave and head back to Virginia from Southeast DC. In the car, Jamie, John, and Eve joke and laugh about how crazy the experience was. They relish in the adrenaline rush. John puts his hand on my thigh as if to remind me that he loves me. All I can do is stare at the glow of the Washington Monument. All I can do is try to fixate on the light.

The cop taps on the window. He grins and hands me back my license. "Good thing it was me that pulled you over. Some aren't as lenient. I'm going to let you off with a warning. Here's your paperwork." He waves and walks back to the car.

I adjust the rearview mirror to make sure that the cop is gone. As he pulls away, my anxiety subsides. I stare at the piece of paper in my hand. FAILURE TO STOP and RECKLESS DRIVING peer back as the reasons as to why I was stopped. But this isn't what immediately catches my eye. It is *his* label. RACE: BLACK. Without looking at my name. Without asking me my ethnicity. One man looked at my skin and read me. This paper told me what I had known all along. My Black body was asking to be harassed. It was deemed reckless for taking up space on the road.

This is how we are born. Through trauma, we stay woke.

LESSON THREE:
LOVE WILL FIND YOU
EVEN IN THE DARK

GBA ARA RE LÀ

There was this glory-looking young woman in the time when animals talked the language of the Motherland. Birdie was every bit her father's child. She, the same opaque Blackness, and hair as fine as silk, was considered a treasured beauty. And she was always saying, "I ain't want for no marked and wounded man." Said it all the time to the boys who came courting.

And then there was *that* animal. The one everybody called Big Ol' Bear. His fur was black onyx that showed brown in the sun and could trick the eyes through its magic.

One day Bear heard Birdie carrying on down by a creek in the woods. She was brushing her hair and singing. With each new tune she'd pluck the black and white feathers out of her tresses like they were grey hairs. Bear thought Birdie was pretty and decided to turn himself into a man and win her heart. He was gonna make her his.

First, he had to look the part. Bear went to a nearby house where an old couple lived. He rapped on the door. Tap. Tap. Tap. Old Woman answered the door and before she could open her mouth, one swipe of Bear's paw knocked her down. Bear stole their clothes and took them to his cave. He practiced for days—standing on hind legs, he'd strut around his cave in pants and a buttoned-up shirt and tie. He stumbled with every step in his shoes. He figured he didn't need no shoes. He saw himself as proper, so he took them off.

One day Birdie went down to the creek for her daily afternoon respite and saw a man fishing. He stood, stumbled, and bowed. "G'day, miss." He removed his cap. Birdie eyed the man up and down. He seemed handsome enough, with a nice shirt, tie, and pants on. All he seemed to be missing was…his shoes.

"G'day," she responded. "What brings you out this way?"

"Oh, the weather's so nice, and I figured it was perfect for catchin a meal. I live alone, see, and sometimes, I get so lonely, and fishin takes my mind off things. If I had a pretty girl like you around, I'd consider that better than anythin I'd catch out here."

The man collected his things. "Well, ma'am. Be seeing you!" With another bow and the tip of his cap he went off into the woods.

Birdie was intrigued. The man *seemed* nice. A good head on his shoulders, but where were his shoes? Birdie sat and sang by the creek. She plucked out more black and white feathers and bathed in the sun. After she was tired, she packed up her blanket and picnic basket and went home. That night she dreamed of flying.

Meanwhile, Ol' Bear knew he had laid his trap. In his cave, he danced and rolled around just beside himself for fooling Birdie that he was human. He knew he had to make her his and would do so soon. It was just a matter of time.

Next, he had to pretend to be the part. Bear went back to the near-by house where the old couple lived. He rapped on the door. Tap. Tap. Tap. Old Man answered the door and before he could open his mouth, one swipe of Bear's paw knocked him down. Bear dressed up in the old man's clothes, stole his car, and drove back to the cave.

The next morning, Birdie and her family went to church. She said her hellos to family friends. George, a boy about her age brought her a flower.

"Pretty girl deserves pretty things," he bowed as he handed her a daisy.

Birdie took the flower and put it in her hair. "Why thank you George! What a fine friend and gentleman you are."

George crumbled under the weight of her words. He hadn't hoped to be just a "friend." Nevertheless, he bowed to her again, and went inside to find a good pew. If he were to win the affections of Birdie, George knew he had to pray on it.

While standing outside on the steps with her mother and George before service, a car drove up to the church and parked right in front. The man from the creek stepped out and adjusted his tie. He dusted off his shoes, and once he saw Birdie and her mother, he tipped his hat and went inside the church house.

"Phewie, that's a fine-looking man," said Birdie's mother.

Birdie nodded and agreed, "And he goes to service, too? That's a good Christian if I ever saw one. Right there. That is the young gentleman I will marry."

Well, Ol' Bear and Birdie did marry, and he carried her right there to the car, he did. They went back through the forest, past the old couple's home, and to Bear's cave. He put Birdie there. "Now that you're my wife, you'll stay here," he told her, "and stay here till I come back."

Well, Bear left her there in that damp dark cave without a scrap to eat or a pot to piss in. He left her there with just one mosquito to mind her, too. And he told that mosquito, "Uh gwine away," and ordered if any man bothers his Birdie to come and tell him.

The mosquito buzzed, "Yassa boss! E tell'um say if 'e kumbayah."

Birdie stayed in that cave for three whole days and nights. There was nothing in that cave except for some berries, some old fish carcasses, and a big, cracked skull that Bear had left.

Now this is true. One day, George was out hunting and found some bear tracks and footprints. He followed them to a cave where inside he heard someone weeping. To his shock he found Birdie there— just as beautiful as ever—but dirty and looking half-dead and whole scared. She told George, "I married this fellow, and he brought me here—don't know why."

Young boy George told her, "I saw his tracks and yours. He may stand upright, but he's not a man. He's a bear!" Birdie nearly fell over. She didn't know what to do. George told her, "You rest up. Come three days, I'll come back to save you." Birdie agreed and George went on his way. Before long, dusk came.

Meanwhile, Mosquito rushed to tell Bear of the goings on. "Big Boss! Big Boss! Mah hed leab me. Mens kumbayah!"

"E tru?" asked Ol' Bear.

"Ah tru mout," replied Mosquito.

Bear ran back to the cave and found Birdie by herself just crying and dirty…but alone. He turned to Mosquito. "Wah side e is?" Before Mosquito could respond, Bear smacked him with his paw.

"Birdie," Bear ordered his wife, "make me some supper."

"But," she squeaked, "there's nothing to eat here…"

In anger, Bear raised his paw and slashed it across Birdie's back and ripped her dress.

"Fine. If you can't feed me, then I'll find it myself." He turned to Mosquito. "Uh gwine away. Tell me if thems mens kumbayah."

Mosquito buzzed, "Yassa boss! E tell'um say if 'e kumbayah."

And with that, Ol' Bear went back into the forest. Meanwhile Birdie tried to distract herself from the pain. She sang and tried to pluck feathers out of her hair. And then, she felt a hand on her back.

"Po' Child," said a voice. "You let that brute do this to you?"

Birdie turned and saw the face of an old woman.

"I ain't done nothing. But I don't know what to do. This Bear tricked me, and now I'm stuck in this cave."

"Child," said the woman, "you ain't stuck. You just gotta learn that trickster's language. I may have let this Bear trick me and take me and my husband's life but not no more. Here's what you do. Take these berries and these fish bones and make him a stew. It'll make him so sick, he won't bother you."

Before Birdie could thank the woman, she disappeared. Birdie did what she was told and put the berries and fish bones into a pot. She told Mosquito to go down to the river to fetch some water for her stew. Before long, Bear came back.

"Birdie," Bear ordered his wife, "make me some supper."

Birdie gathered some stew and put it into the skull. Bear slurped it down, every morsel. Then, his stomach started to rumble. He started to feel real sick.

"Ah!" He screamed. "You poisoned me, woman!"

"I sure did," said Birdie. "And the Ol' Lady said, 'E tell 'um say 'i hafsah do 'um.'"

Shocked at the girl's last words the Bear exclaimed, "You crack 'e teet of our langwidge."

Birdie smiled and replied, "Sho' do. Been here long enuf I l'aan. Yo wunt git bettuh o' me no mo'!"

Then Ol' Bear says, "Well Birdie, you can go on and leave. I won't hurt you no more. I just married you to let you know that a woman can't be more than a man. Because you said you wouldn't marry a young man who was marked and wounded. I tricked you to show you how you didn't know everything." Then Bear got on all four legs and ran off into the woods.

"Phew," Birdie said. "Glad that's over." Birdie dusted herself off and left the cave.

There in the forest, she found George. He was surprised as he hadn't gotten far enough to town to get supplies to rescue her, but he hugged her all the same.

As he wrapped her up in his coat, he whispered in her ear, "I may not have saved you, but I will make sure no one ever will hurt you again." He took Birdie's hand and guided her home. Sometime later they got married and for the fifty years following George would be the salve on Birdie's wounds.

Pretty Fly

*"**I would understand** if you left me for a Black guy. I just know that I can never fully support you in the ways you need because I'm white."*

Where is this coming from?

I look at Nick. The sides of his brown eyebrows always point together when he's insecure. Insecurity, after all, is the mothafucka of doubt and doubt is the mothafucka of all logic.

The creases in his forehead form like folds of fresh dough. I want to knead them into something new. I want to tell him that one of the most common questions people ask me is why I only date white guys. I want to tell him that my parents swore it was a phase. I want to tell him that his assumptions couldn't be further from the truth. Instead, I try to smile. I grimace, as if to ease the tension between us. I hold his hand and put his head on my chest. I tell him I love him. I laugh off the concern as some joke. It's far easier to settle in the margins of the punchline.

The difference between our skin tones is always pointed out to me as if I'm colorblind. As if I'm ignorant to certain truths. Truth is, Black women are statistically more unlikely to date outside of their race. Black women are also statistically ranked as the least desirable demographic in online dating pools. Black women are also ranked as most unlikely to marry.

Out of the seventy-some people I've had sex with, only three have been Black. Sixty-eight percent of white cis-males I've had sex with gave me the following post-coital feedback: "I can't believe I just had sex with a Black girl!" Calling me a "Nubian Queen" at climax is also a frequent utterance.

My fondest and perhaps most disturbing memory was when a white Jewish partner asked if I would call him a "kike" during sex. While I am always open to kinks, I refused him. I knew he was hoping to return the same derogatory favor. He wanted permission to say it.

But these truths are things I cannot relay to Nick. I don't want to out of fear that these utterances will eventually scare him or even worse, make him feel sorry for me. I also refuse to face these truths for fear of acknowledging the more embarrassing parts of myself.

Quiet as it's kept, I dated a Black man once. And I made damn sure he was
Blackity
Black
BLACK.

It was Christmas. Driving to Pittsburgh in his Chrysler 300, me and this Howard University alum listened to music and joked. Probably even smoked a jay or two on the four-hour drive to my parents' house. And it was nice. My parents made dinner. There was laughter and my Dad called him *brotha* but beyond that I can't remember much.

What I do remember fondly is taking a stroll along the bike path that ran parallel to the Monongahela River, the air being so crisp the wind sliced my chapped lips and nose. I remember Louis and I laughing, holding hands, the sound of mud and small stones crunching underfoot.

When our walk was complete, and we re-entered my parents' home from such a nice romantic stroll, I remember opening the door and seeing my parents high fiving. I remember my mother hugging Louis and my father saying, "Come back *anytime,* man." I broke up with Louis shortly after that. My parents still reminisce of Louis fondly as if he is dead or was their last great hope of having a Black son-in-law—even though he is now happily married and has a kid somewhere in Maryland.

"What do you find most attractive about white men?" my therapist asks.

I sit with this question. Let it bounce back and forth between synapses before I respond. "I don't think I'm more so attracted to white men as much as my trauma is more deeply rooted with Black men."

I excuse the triggers away. My real father for never being a part of my life. My stepfather's abuse when he drinks. My cousin sexually abusing me for eight years. My uncle who refuses to name his son as a "rapist" by giving his actions a less harmful name: "incest." My other cousin calling me a liar, threatening to kill me, and boasting of how easily I could "disappear."

As soon as I let these words escape my lips to my therapist, I already know they are a copout. Trauma—for Black women—is inherited.

Pussy Prayers: Sacred and Sensual Rituals for Wild Women of Color says that many of our sexual beliefs stem from our ancestors and from the enslavement of African people in America, where: "In a time and place where women had their identity and autonomy violently stolen, having no control over where their daughters or they themselves would be taken, forced and ravaged at the will of white plantation owners, our foremothers developed a way to cope."

I think about these words often when I think about the women in my family. I think about the ways my family dismisses pain like it's sweeping dust bunnies under the couch. I think about the ways my mother asks me about therapy recommendations like she's asking for my advice about a dildo.

I think about my Aunt Bert's first ex-husband. It wouldn't be until years later that she told me about the day she decided to leave him. How she sat at the side of the bed as he slept holding a butcher knife, praying for celestial hands to intervene. The next day, after a therapist told her that she needed medication, Aunt Bert destroyed his office. She went home to pack her things and purchased a revolver with a pearl handle to keep by her nightstand. A revolver she threatened to shoot her sister's ex-husband with after he laid hands on my Aunt Geneva.

I think about my Aunt Carole's words that now refrain like a Gospel hymn: "We are family, after all." Shit. The women in my family have been coping for centuries.

Perhaps my preference for white men is a reclamation of sexual power.

Perhaps I'm taking back my autonomy through my sexual exploits.

Perhaps I'm just disconnected from my body.

Perhaps I am just a race traitor.

"Did you not have bad experiences with white men?" My best friend's husband, Kevin, asks me during a phone call where she's put me on speaker.

Together, Makai and I go through the list. Mike, my high school boyfriend, had stalked me senior year because I dumped him. I had to get a restraining order. Paul knocked me up and got me hooked on cocaine after I had an abortion. Steve would pick and choose when he'd want to spend time with me, hit on my girlfriends when I wasn't around, and kept a bag of other women's lingerie in his wardrobe like they were trophies. John gave me a black eye on Valentine's Day when he was convinced that I was cheating on him because *he* wasn't being faithful. Jorge never wanted to work, was content living with his mother in a trailer park, and ended up leaving me for a white girl. I didn't date anyone for five years after that and couldn't have sex without crying.

"I guess the white men in my life weren't much better," I nervously chuckle.

"Yeah," Makai responds, "but you fought back."

And then the epiphany hit me. *Fight.* It was easier to reduce it to something so simple. To forgive the Black men in my life for their transgressions came naturally. It's okay when Men leave you. It's okay for Men to hurt you. You know better than to talk back. You know better than to spill our secrets. You are strong enough to forgive, just don't forget. You will tell these stories in hushed tones on couches over tea in your own time. You will whisper them into folds of casseroles shoved into stoves. Move on for now. Let it go.

Black women are taught to forgive Black men. To survive in this country is hard enough on them. We don't have to forgive white men. We are allowed to be angry. We are allowed to fight. With each of the white men I dated, even when it came to blows and the relationship was toxic, I stood up for myself. In some weird, fucked up way, I felt like I had agency where my relationships with Black men taught me that I had to be submissive. A submission that was drilled into my head over and over again like a mantra, like a prayer. *After all, we are family.*

Nick and I decided to go get ice cream after a movie date. Standing in line, I see my cousin's wife and two of his daughters standing 20 people in front of us. The youngest one meets my eye and a pit in my stomach forms as I duck behind a pillar. I can feel the anxiety swelling up, my heart pounding against my chest as I forget how to breathe.

"Are you alright?" Nick asks.

I shake my head. "My cousin's family is here."

The corners of his mouth turn upward until he realizes who I mean. And like with all triggers the flashes rush in. Nick grabs my hand and leads me to the car. Nick unlocks it, grabs the passenger door, and lifts me inside. As soon as the doors lock, all I can do is scream and cry. All he can do is whisper, "It's okay. It's not your fault. It is night, we are in a parking lot. You are safe."

Once I calm down, he turns on the car and we head home. "That line was too long for some soft serve anyways," Nick tries to reassure me. We take turns playing songs over his Echo Auto that's streaming through the radio of his 2005 Toyota Camry. I put on "Bonfire" by Childish Gambino and Nick nods his head to the beat. Together we sing along, taking each verse in its cadence and rhyme. Nick always spits each lyric perfectly. He knows every word, every syllable, and the pauses verbatim. For the first time in our relationship, I notice something new.

Every time the word "nigga" comes up in the song, Nick omits saying it. It comes like second nature, and he doesn't even stumble. Where most white men dating a Black woman think that gives them agency to say it, Nick makes the choice to abstain.

That vocabulary isn't his, and it never will be. He knows it and protects me from the harm a word like that can produce. He clears his throat.

"Alexa, put on Cam'ron."

Cam. Rahn. His whiteness mangles the name so even Alexa cannot abide his request. He rolls his eyes and puts on Kendrick Lamar instead.

We pass by open fields of farmland. The warmness of the summer breeze whips between my fingertips. Even if I can't reassure him, I know that, like the rapper serenading us in his vehicle says, "We gon' be alright."

Lesson Four:
Persevere and Lay the Groundwork for Others

Sise Taratara

People still talk about the night Archie "Bird" Coles was born. Talk about it all the time. Just like with all good stories, this one starts on a dark and cloudy night.

As snow trickled from the sky, lightning crackled across it. As if by magic, between the roar of thunder and the whirl of wind, Nellie and Jesse welcomed their new son into the world. People ain't never seen something so miraculous. His parents showed him to everyone they met. Archie was the most powerful-looking child they'd ever seen, with thick arms and strong muscles. He continued growing till he was the strongest man who ever lived.

Archie grew up into a world where children like him never stayed children for very long. By the time he was a teenager, he and his brother Silas would go with their daddy to the steel mill. Archie eventually became a steel-working man, just like his daddy. Even still, he was soft like his momma. Never cussed a day in his life. No, this man wouldn't dare hurt a fly. Carrying piles of coal from one smokestack to another, his favorite part was watching the men turn steel into liquid gold. Watching hard, dull, grey metal turn into golden possibility was an enchantment. Molten steel transformed into airplanes, casings for bullets, and foundations for tall buildings downtown.

But then the second World War came, and Archie had to go over-seas to support *his* country. Years passed and while the war was won, Archie had changed. He fought a little harder. Drilled steel and filled the smokestacks with coal a little faster. Eventually Archie met a girl, Bonnie, who was just as pretty as her name. Together they had two daughters and a son.

Archie worked hard day in and day out as the sun rose over the hills of Homestead and the yellow dust mixed with smoke. He'd walk down to that Steel Mill a little more broken each day. But he had little mouths to feed and bills to pay. The bite of liquor swelled in his gut, but he'd smile and go on just the same.

Archie got the reputation of the hardest working man in the mill. He could carry heavy beams of steel like he was picking up a bundle of sticks. He could shovel coal faster and could make the fires in the furnace burn brighter than any man.

Not before too long, the other Black workers started calling Archie "Boss Man Bird," even though he was their equal in pay. He would be the one to talk to the foreman about missing wages. Pick up the slack for the men who got burned or too sick from the fumes of burning metal. All the while he'd smile and say, "I ain't no one's boss. A man ain't nothing but a man."

One day, the foreman asked all the men to gather in the middle of the mill.

"Now listen here," the foreman said. "New machines are coming in today to cut down on the workload around here. Most of the spots are filled but I'm in a tight spot and I need one man. Just one." One of the workers raised his hand. "How 'bout Boss Man Bird? He could do it!"

The men all cheered and clapped.

"Boss man? You mean *Archie?*"

"Yeah, Boss!" The men cheered. "Let Boss Man Bird do it! He's just as good as any white man!"

The foreman spit. "Ain't no Black man better than me. But I'm desperate. Tell you what I do. If Archie agrees to work today, I'll make him a boss tomorrow. *Your* boss." Archie looked around at the nodding heads. He knew new machines meant new unemployment. He knew that even if he was made boss, that meant nothing.

"Tell you what, Boss," said Archie. "If I work today and make the most beams out of anyone here, I want your promise that these men will have jobs tomorrow." The foreman scratched the scruff of his neck, wiped the sweat beading on his forehead and nodded. The men all cheered, and Archie followed the foreman.

On the other side of the mill stood tall blue and yellow machines with hoses attached on both sides. With every crunch of raw steel came a BOOM that shook the ground. Archie had never seen anything like that before.

The foreman pointed to a step ladder in front of the machine, showed him the buttons and the lever. BOOM. He'd put steel in, and BOOM, out came a pressed beam, shiny and new. When he looked for coal, one of the other white machinists chuckled and said that this new machine was electric-operated.

Hours passed. Archie would walk over to the pile of untouched steel, put it in the machine, and BOOM. By the time the whistle blew, and the men climbed down from their perches, Archie just kept going. Pile of steel. Machine. BOOM.

People said they could hear thunder coming from that steel mill. It was like God and the Devil themselves was bowling down by that river.

Before long, morning came, and the men returned to the mill. By the time the foreman found Archie, he had made more than three-hundred steel beams, more than all of the white machinists had made in one day combined. The Black workers cheered. "Boss Man Bird is faster than dynamite during a hurricane!"

The foreman wasn't pleased. "Looks like we got a man full of vinegar here."

Archie replied, "I'm a man. And a man ain't nothing but a man. That's all."

"Well," said the foreman, "let's make a deal. If you can make double this, I'll give you and all your buddies raises and, heck, I'll even buy you lunch!"

Archie looked at his friends, their hardened faces hiding pleading eyes. He knew he didn't have a choice, and nodded to the foreman. "You got yourself a deal, Boss." The Black workers cheered, all patting Archie on the back.

Archie climbed back up his machine and pressed the button. BOOM. Another beam down. And again, he worked and worked. By the time the whistle blew, and the men climbed down from their perches, Archie stayed. Just humming to himself, *This little light of mine...*BOOM...*I'm gonna let it shine...*BOOM...*This little light of mine...*BOOM.

People said they could hear thunder down at that steel mill. It was like God and the Devil themselves was bowling down by that river, but this time, the Devil lost. God had bowled a perfect game.

Before long, morning came, and the men returned to the mill. By the time the foreman found Archie, there were more than seven hundred steel beams down by his station. The men all cheered as Archie climbed down. "Now Boss, a deal's a deal. Give these men what's owed, and I'll be on my way."

"But Archie," claimed the foreman, "the day's not done. You ain't going anywhere just yet."

The Black workers booed. One of them jeered, "Aw, c'mon, Boss! Give the poor guy a break!"

The foreman wasn't having it. Poor Archie climbed back the ladder and pushed the button. BOOM.

By the time the whistle blew, Archie could barely lift his arms. Working three days straight was hard on any man, let alone a man as strong as Archie. As the foreman promised, he gave all the men their raise. He handed Archie a half-eaten sandwich which Archie couldn't stomach.

By the time he got home to his Bonnie, he dropped his hard hat and fell to his knees. Bonnie cradled him in her arms.

"That machine took my place, but I did beat it. And other machines are coming to take other mens' places, but I got them what's owed nonetheless."

Bonnie kissed her husband's forehead. "You ain't gotta prove nothing to no man, Bird. Let's fly away from here before they kill you."

Archie and Bonnie packed up their things. They sent their kids off to find proper schooling. They were going to head west. West a man could manifest his *own* future. As the last of their things were packed in the trunk and hood of their car, the first and only Black man in Pittsburgh to work that machine drove off into the sunset.

MisEducation

Dear Black Girl,

No one is going to teach you how to love your body. In fact, you most likely are going to spend a lifetime with others in your life trying to police it. They feel entitled to comment on the way your body performs. They judge the way it takes up space. Expect to be a fetish. Expect at times to feel unseen and unheard. Expect to be a "token." Expect to be that "one Black friend." Expect to be an "other." Expect to feel replaceable. Expect to feel disposable.

Babygirl, no one is going to teach you about the nuances of melanin. Between the praxis of "haves and have nots," between dark skinned to red boned to just plain ol' high yella, the world is going to seek to define you. It is going to line your hue up against food and make you mocha, coffee, or caramel. This is the paradox of being a Black woman.

The miasma that is you is going to evolve unequivocally. You'll learn with time that your hair is both your superpower and your Achilles' heel. Your origin story starts from the time that coils form on the top of your crown. It begins on top of kitchen sink basins with mothers, grandmothers, and aunties on washdays. These are the first women who'll stick their fingers in between the strands of your hair to measure its *goodness*. Good hair is and will always be the goal.

You can remember the thick, sulphureous smell of hot metal burning against your hair follicles. The glob of the Blue Magic hair jelly sliding across each outlined part in your scalp cools your flesh. The tug of your mother's hand that yanks on the next unmanageable strand of hair is utter agony. She squeezes your ribcage with her thighs and tells you to "hold still." She calls you *tender-headed*. As she sets the hot comb with the wooden handle back on the burner, she grabs the curling iron. With the flick of her wrist and a clickety-clack, each stroke of the heat on each strand feels straighter with the passing minutes.

And you *feel* cute. With your curly-Q tresses and matching purple shirt and bow you gap-tooth grin extra wide for the photographer that's taking your third-grade photo. The photographer pauses, grabs a comb, and walks towards you. They intend to fix that one strand that doesn't seem to lay down. And with a gasp you see a curly strand of your hair attached to the comb and both you and the photographer are puzzled by this immediate hair loss. You put the strand of hair in your pocket. Take it home to your mother and show her in an open palm. "Shit. Maybe I put too much heat on your hair," she concludes. "You just wanted it *so* straight…" This, you remember, is your first lesson with your hair.

Your second lesson comes from a toy. For Christmas you ask your mother for an American Girl doll. "That one," you point to in the catalog, the one with the *nice* hair. Your Addy doll may be Black, like you, but the coarseness of her hair, the way it never braids and scratches your little fingers, feels wrong. It isn't manageable. It isn't pretty. Josefina is brown, like you, has glossy hair that hangs limp and can fold into French braids with ease. Josefina has a birthday. She wasn't born a slave or an only child.

Josefina is a revolutionary in the advent of war where Addy was just another Black girl who ran from the plantation where she was born to find freedom. A child doesn't understand the strength it takes to take flight. She doesn't understand the risk. She doesn't want a doll that looks like her. She dreams of a girl with light skin and *good* hair like her white friends.

At this moment you are ten, and it takes about two decades for American Girl to change the texture of Addy's hair. You discover this through a Google search in your 30s. The shock of seeing the silky texture of what Addy's hair is now makes you angry. You mourn for both you and your former doll's scalps.

You can remember the first time you get a relaxer. The way the cream mixed with chemicals smells suspicious to an unsuspecting tween—or, as your mother calls it, "that sweet spot between childhood and adolescence." The burn on your scalp isn't just in one or two places. Your whole head feels like someone walked up behind you and lit a match. You project yourself away from your mother's tightening thigh lock and scream, running to the bathroom. Behind you your mother screams, "You wanted this," and, "This is how your hair will get straight!"

When you wash out the cream, you remember the smell of the shampoo and conditioner and feel disappointed by its pungent malodor. The products that claimed to smell like apples on the box instead smell like rotten eggs. You remember the sores, how the water on your raw scalp came as a relief. You don't care about the scabs that form. Your hair is straight. Your hair can flip like a white girl's. This is when you learn the mantra and will continue to remind yourself for years to follow that "beauty knows no pain."

You remember seventh grade. The moments when you'd wear your hair in ponytails and girls like Ashlee and Porsche would pull your hair in gym class. Between sobs and between her thighs, your mother would brush your hair. As she French braided it, she'd explain. "Not all girls can grow their hair like you."

At first, this comment confuses you. You, the girl who thinks her hair is ugly and can never seem to be straight enough. This is when you discover things called weaves. This is when you understand the word "extension." This is when you decide to wear your hair in buns to hide its length. But it is too late. Your hair, your long straight silky relaxed hair connotes whiteness because it's as malleable as dolls'. By the end of middle school your classmates nickname you "Boobless Barbie" and "Oreo." By high school your skin grows as thick as your hair.

Your fourth lesson on hair doesn't come until your first semester away at college. For decades you relied on your mother's arthritic hands to tame your tresses. Before long the roughness of your natural roots begins to sprout. No matter how much heat or how many minutes you hold the straightening iron on your strands, the bump of new growth won't lay flat. You eventually ask your girlfriend Tiara to give you a perm. After all, she reminds you, she has younger sisters and does this all the time.

In the Korean hair store she asks you what brand of relaxer you use and again you panic because your mom usually makes these decisions on your behalf. You only know of the brand based on the woman on the box. It's pink and the woman rocks a bob with a come-hither look. You reduce the options to two kinds: Regular and Super. Tiara combs through your hair and thumbs the strands. "You got a pretty thick head," she tells you. You both decide that it must be Super.

The thighs of a Black woman are a homegoing. Tieara's hips are invitingly warm. Like your mother's, her thighs squeeze the sides of your shoulders. She parts your hair into four sections like your mother, too. She mixes the pink chemical into the cream and uses the wooden spatula to stir. She applies the cream from the back and works her way forward. At first, you feel that familiar burn. It tingles first, but then, three minutes in, it starts to burn. And not just burn, it is on FIRE.

You tell yourself that beauty knows no pain. You jiggle your leg and try to do deep breathing. By the time T is done, you run to the shower stalls. You wash the cream out. You add neutralizing shampoo, but the burn is excruciating. It rages on. Then you notice that hair is falling out. And it's not just a strand here or there but whole clumps on all sides of your head. By the time you finish your shower, you look in the mirror. Your hair is straight alright, but your once-voluminous shoulder-length mane is gone. The hair that once could be pulled neatly into a donut-sized bun is now reduced to a limply mop that hangs a bit past your ear lobes.

In horror, you'll notice baby hairs on the sides of your temples are now bright-red patches of skin. This is when you learn the term *bald-headed.* This is when you learn to improvise. For the two years following when people comment on your hair, expect to lie. Tell them the bob you rock was completely intentional. Years later you will learn that the iconic Salt-n-Pepa asymmetrical hairstyle was the result of a tragic hair mistake, too. In this you will learn that embarrassing hairstyles are a part of growth.

In the decade to follow, you will continue to get relaxers. You are conditioned, after all, to rely on that creamy crack. You don't care if prolonged use turns your scalp green. As long as you can style your hair like your white friends, none of it matters. But then something happens when you turn 30. Your half-white, half-Mexican boyfriend leaves you for a white woman. You compare yourself to her. You wonder if you were white, would he have stayed? You question, would dating—in general—be easier?

You take some time to find yourself. You start to focus on your career and life ambitions and start to read more books by Black writers. You start to build resolve. You decide to reset from head to toe. After years of buying products that never seem to smooth your hair down just right, years of scabbed scalps and ear and forehead burns from straightening irons, the fight with your hair and the longing to look white grows tiresome.

You resolve that your hair will never be as straight or as limp as any white girl's. You start to befriend more Black girls like you, and they rock curly, textured hair. The way it coils and still flips and bounces is mesmerizing. You wish your hair could look like that.

You see girls with shaved heads and dreadlocks, and you begin to wonder if your hair can do those things, too. Things your mother was doing all along.

You start your natural hair journey in 2018. You let your relaxer grow out and try new things like twists and bantu knots. You look up YouTube video after video trying to find instructions on how to style your hair. You start to rock braids, and on bad hair days, you rock bandanas like you're a Black Rosie the Riveter. A year in, your hair routine becomes second nature. Wash day, twists, hair bonnet, Repeat. Your white friends start to comment on your hair change. Your new curly hair seems exotic and exciting for them. They feel compelled to touch it. Your friends of color applaud you for your commitment.

A random visit to your former hairdresser leads to what you hear is called *the big chop*. With each snip of the shear, the traumas interwoven through those tresses are untethered. You watch as the last of what remains falls away. Your coily canvas is now reborn. You and your hair are now a blank slate.

That summer you use bandanas and head wraps to hold your coily afro out of your face. One day, you're at DSW with your mom looking at Timberlands that you told her you wanted as a birthday present. "The Black ones," you tell her. The ones that aren't that cliché construction beige. While in the checkout line, the cashier—a Black girl—looks at your hair. "Your hair is so pretty. I wish my hair could do that," she tells you. "I'm just so afraid to do the big chop."

Like second nature, you tell her what products you use. You instruct her on what styles worked best when you *transitioned*. For the first time in your life, you embrace your hair for what it is and feel pride. You find new strength and resiliency in each coil your burned and chemically altered strands never afforded you. You learn that there is beauty in nature. You learn that you are not your hair.

Lesson Five:
Feed Your Mind
to Nourish Your Soul

SISE LATI OKAN

Black folks talk about the magic of Gillie Coles' cauldron.

White folks talk about her, too.

Every kind of folk claim her as kin, and there are good reasons why.

Let me tell you...

Once upon a time, not yours or mine, but a bygone time, some people was owned. And the owners were called Master and Mistress. And no matter what, the owners knew what the owned were doing. Knew what time they needed to be in the fields. Knew what time they were allowed to pray. Knew the goings on upon the land they owned and gave a name to everything that lived on it. Nothing ever happened without Master and Mistress' say so.

Aunt Becky was to be married. Aunt Becky, you see, took care of Master and Mistress' babies. Nursed them as soon as they took their first breath and raised them right by the time they could walk, even though she never had one for her own. By some time, Master made an agreement with his neighbor that Becky could marry any man of the neighbor's choosing. Both men could make a profit in having a wedding. Becky could work on both farms and she could make babies for Master to sell. But today was Becky's day, and Master said the owned could take the afternoon off to celebrate as good Christians are wont to do.

And it was gonna be a *fine* affair. The womenfolk took Becky and made her a beautiful dress of lace. They laughed and giggled in one of the nearby cabins as they fit her for her garments. They piled her hair up and stuck it full of magpie feathers to match the dress. Some of the younger ones picked wildflowers and made Aunt Becky a crown and braided the crown with ribbons every color of the rainbow. The menfolk fashioned an altar with a garland. They built benches for the elders so they could sit in peace. Oh yes, it was gonna be a *fine* affair.

Gillie was Master and Mistress' cook, and their favorite one at that. She could make anything taste like Heaven. One bite of her food, people said, and you'd never want another morsel made by hands that weren't hers. For Becky's wedding she told herself she was gonna make a feast to feed every mouth, but to do so, she knew she had to ask Master and Mistress first.

After serving Master and Mistress every meal by hand, Gillie also was the one responsible for clearing their plates. After breakfast that morning, Gillie cleared their plates like always.

"Another fine meal, Gillie," said Master. "Another great start to the day."

"Why thank you, Master and Mistress," Gillie replied. "And on a day like today it's important that we all get our strength."

Master sat back and rubbed his belly. "Today? What's happening today?"

"The wedding, dear," replied Mistress, "Today is Becky's special day. Our girl is becoming a woman." Master took another sip of his coffee.

"Yes! Thank you, wife. I completely forgot. Becky is your kin isn't she, Gillie?"

"Oh yes," Gillie responded bashfully. "I'd like to make a feast for the celebration, with your permission, of course." Master looked at his wife and took another sip.

Mistress touched her husband's hand.

"Oh, please dear! It could be a wedding present from us!"

"Well," he started, "I don't see the harm. As long as it doesn't take away from your work. Take two chickens from the coop. That should be more than enough to feed everyone." With that, the Master waved Gillie off. She bowed to Master and Mistress and took the plates into the kitchen. *Two chickens?* Gillie thought. *That wouldn't nearly feed half of us.*

By and by, the owned came from the neighboring farm along with Becky's promised man, Beau. With them they brought one chicken and some pig guts to add to the feast. Gillie went to the coop and killed and plucked two chickens. She fried as much as she could and left the carcasses on the counter. Even though she had about two buckets of chicken, there were fifty mouths to feed. Even with the chitterlings, she still needed more.

Gillie went to the forest to find fresh huckleberries to pick for pies. She picked and picked till her fingers turned purple and her apron was full. On her way back to the kitchen she saw a turtle spinning on its back.

"Please help me," Brer Turtle begged. "Some folk done kicked me over and now I can't get up."

"Poor Brer Turtle. I'll help you," Gillie replied. She leaned over and, with one hand, turned Brer Turtle right side up. "There, there," Gillie said.

Brer Turtle smiled. He stood on his hind legs and bowed. His stomach rumbled. "Please help me," Brer Turtle begged. "I was laying there for so long I worked up a hunger."

"Poor Brer Turtle. I'll help you," Gillie replied. Gillie reached into her apron and handed the turtle some berries she was saving. "There, there." Brer Turtle grabbed the berries and stuffed them into his beak. When he was done, he bowed again.

"Well, thank you, kind woman. You helped me, now, what can I do for you?"

"Oh, I don't want for nothing. Just want to make a feast for my kin's wedding. I'm surely worried that I won't have enough food to feed everyone, especially now that I gave you all of them berries."

Brer Turtle took off his shell. "Take this. Put this and some bones into a pot. It'll make the finest soup you've ever tasted. Better yet, every time you spoon some out, more will fill in the pot in its place."

Gillie took the turtle's shell. "Why, thank you!" Brer Turtle bowed, and with that, he walked away. Gillie ripped some of her dress and made a knapsack for the shell. She continued to walk towards the farm till she found a rabbit with his foot in a trap.

"Please help me," Brer Rabbit begged. "Some men done tricked me and now I can't get out."

"Poor Brer Rabbit, I'll help you," Gillie replied. Gillie leaned over and, with one hand, untied the string around Brer Rabbit's foot. "There, there." Brer Rabbit stood on his hind legs and bowed. His stomach rumbled. "Please help me," Brer Rabbit begged. "I was laying there for so long I worked up a hunger."

"Poor Brer Rabbit. I'll help you," Gillie replied. Gillie reached into her apron and handed Brer Rabbit the last of her berries she was saving. "There, there." Brer Rabbit grabbed the berries and stuffed them into his mouth. When he was done, he bowed again.

"Well, thank you, kind woman. You helped me, now, what can I do for you?"

"Oh, I don't want for nothing. Just want to make a feast for my kin's wedding. I'm surely worried that I won't have enough food to feed everyone, especially now that I gave you the last of my berries. I was going to make some pies."

Brer Rabbit smiled and hopped over to a sage bush. He gathered up the branches, whispered into his paws, and handed them to Gillie.

"Take this. If you put these and some apples into some dough, it'll make the finest cake you've ever tasted. Better yet, every time you cut a slice, more will fill on the plate in its place."

Gillie took the sage and put it into her apron. "Why, thank you!" Brer Rabbit bowed and with that he hopped away. Time was cutting close, and Gillie still had work to do. She continued back towards the farm to cook as she was told.

First, she made the stew. She took the Brer Turtle's shell and threw the chicken bones into the pot and filled it with water. She added some salt and pepper, some vegetables, and sure enough, just like Brer Turtle had promised, the stew became thick and overflowing with chicken and turtle meat.

Then, she made the cake. She went to the apple orchard and picked the juiciest and reddest apples she could find. She sliced the fruit and took the sage and folded it into batter. She put the cake pan into the oven. Just like Brer Rabbit had promised, out came the biggest and sweetest smelling cake Gillie had ever seen. She covered the cake with brown sugar and put it back in the oven to glaze. When the cake and the stew were done, Gillie asked the menfolk to carry the food outside.

People say Aunt Becky's wedding was the best affair. Said it for years to come. Becky and Beau jumped the broom. When they crossed, Becky hugged her cousin and took the magpie feathers and put them in Gillie's hair. People danced and ate until their bellies were full. For one full day they forgot that they was owned.

And it was a *fine* feast indeed.

BATTER UP

"Come here," my mother instructs me. "Lean in close over the stove." I walk over to the cast iron skillet. The warmth of the Crisco mixed with butter smells salty and sweet. The sizzle, the crackling whispers of the chicken, reverberate through me. I hear the POP and back away before the hot oil catches on my skin and clothes. "That," my mother says half-smiling, "is how you know the chicken is done."

My family's love language has always been food.

My earliest memory of fried chicken is at Grandmother's house on Sundays. Her thin, frail forearm turned chicken with a fork. Each piece was always goldened to perfection, as if it came from the store. The battered skin crunched between my teeth and burned the roof of my mouth. She'd call me "Pretty Miss" and stroke my forehead. Later, in bed together, I would snuggle up next to her under the comforter as she cross-stitched her next masterpiece and watch David Letterman. I would fall asleep to the sound of her teeth against the flesh of a wing hidden in a napkin. That was my lullaby, the crunch of my grandmother's teeth. Her dentures against bone were my white noise.

After my Grandmother's passing, my mother still made fried chicken on Sundays. She'd stand over the same cast iron pan that was once her mother's and turn the chicken occasionally with a fork. As she fried, she'd have me wash and clean the collard greens mixed with kale. Together over the hot stove of boiling ham hocks and the sizzling serenade of frying poultry, we'd dance and sing to Stevie Wonder. *Isn't she lovely? Isn't she made from God?*

In my mother's cooking there was home. There was warmth. There was comfort. Together in the kitchen my mother taught me the alchemy of my ancestry that my grandmother had taught to her.

Historically, most fried chicken recipes come from Black women. These were your mammies and your house cooks. The women who, after they were no longer enslaved, stayed to bring their former masters warm meals out of pity and misplaced loyalty. These are the women who became entrepreneurs and sold their fried chicken at train stations and at roadside stands for white people passing by. They were the ones whose recipes were stolen, altered, and circulated into fast food chains.

I think about this every time I see a Popeyes commercial, the way a Black woman on the TV legitimizes the fact that a white man from Louisiana started a fried chicken franchise. I think about Miss Childress, the Black woman who sold her recipe to Colonel Sanders for a measly $1,200. I wonder how many stories we've never heard. I wonder how many battles are lost before they exit Black women's kitchens.

When it comes to fried chicken, I too have battled with white men.

With time, tinkering, and temperance, my fried chicken recipe and my ability to cook it came with a sense of pride. With each batch mixed with seasoned salt and pepper, I perfected my mother's alchemy into a new creation. Old Bay for my Maryland upbringing. A bit of honey whisked with egg and buttermilk to soak my meat in. But no matter what seasonings I use, the process is always as my mother taught me. It comes, an astral whisper over my shoulder:

> *fill a plastic grocery bag with seasonings and flour*
> *shake till chicken is covered*
> *put it on a plate*
> *check if the oil is hot enough*
> *drip a bit of water on it from the faucet*
> **flick hand**
> *if it crackles, then throw in that bird*
> *once you hear the chicken POP*
> *you'll know it's done*
> *put it in a bowl—*
> *make sure there's paper towel lining to catch the drippings*
> *otherwise, you'll have soggy chicken*

In grad school there was a friendly fried chicken cook-off between me and some friends. It was a battle royale where, over stove tops and deep fryers, Nicole, (bi-racial but Black) and Johnny, (a white boy from West Virginia) and I competed to see who the ultimate chicken fryer was. We had a panel of judges. We had our respective corners.

Johnny was even nice enough to supply the chicken. Moving to some consanguineous rhythm, I channel my mother's process: plastic bag, seasonings, flour. But then, as the oil warmed and the bag was prepped and buttermilk was poured into the bowl, I noticed that the only chicken Johnny had left to use was… boneless and skinless breasts.

BONELESS. SKINLESS. BREASTS.

I did the best with what I had. I poked holes into the chicken to let the buttermilk seep in. I shook the meat in the plastic bag with seasoning and flour a little longer and harder.

When the chicken was done frying, we put our creations on a plate before the three judges. Then, I noticed Johnny's plate. A leg, two wings, and one thigh.

Naturally, Johnny won the competition. I came in second and Nicole, third. I was shocked that my recipe—a recipe passed down through generations—lost. I felt like an embarrassment to my ancestors. A recipe I had worked so hard to perfect meant nothing in comparison to a white man's meal. I made a meal that had been judged. It was rendered less than.

With time, I learned to forgive myself. I realized that I was never meant to win. Not really. The cook-off was my first lesson on privilege. It was learning how to take the leftovers of a white man and make do with what was given. It was the same song and story of my ancestors. I was born into a world where my people made masterpieces of pig knuckles and intestines.

Historically, chicken is a staple in many Black families as it was a cheap way to feed the enslaved. Sundays were the only days in which slaves were allowed to spend some modicum of leisure with family, and on these days, fried chicken was often made. There is a sense of ownership that comes from fried chicken. A sense of pride that the same meals that sustained my preceding lineage still continue to feed my family. I can make greens, Hoppin John on New Year's, and sweet potato pie, but my fried chicken is the staple that tethers me to my Black kin.

My great-great-great grandmother, Gillie Coles, was an enslaved cook. Day in and day out, she fed the white folk and nourished their stomachs. How many tears did Gillie cough back over stirred pots? How many kitchen floors did my grandmother scrub on bruised knees?

I think about this every time I cook for white friends and loved ones. I cook as an act of love, and, yet sometimes I worry that all the work of my foremothers was in vain. On those days where I sweat over steaming pots of collard greens, a double consciousness unveils: I am doing exactly what they were *forced* to do. I am no better than a Mammy. I am no better than a coon. I am stereotype incarnate.

Some days, though, being a stereotype is both beautiful and bittersweet.

The day that it was announced that Kamala Harris would be the first woman and person of color as the 49th Vice President of the United States, Nicole and I celebrated.

Twerking to Beyoncé and flipping our natural hair around us, we danced in jubilee at the possibilities that Black girls like us could be magical. It didn't matter if we witnessed countless Black lives being snuffed out in the year of a plague of racism and ignorance.

It didn't matter that the pandemic forced us all into isolation or challenged us to question what value relationships held in our lives;

in that moment, all that mattered was we had survived in spite of a system designed for girls like Nicole and I to fail.

Over Nicole's cast iron skillet, the chicken sizzled while waffles cooked to a perfect golden crust. Braless in our pajamas, we tossed back Jell-O shots and sang "Who Runs the World" and "Diva." Beyoncé reminded us why Black women are the epitome of excellence. I flipped the chicken with a fork. I listened for the POP. When the food was done, we plated our beautiful meals and sat on Nicole's couch. Nicole turned to me and smiled.

"I love us," she sighed, pouring maple syrup over her plate.

"I know," I replied. "We are pretty great."

In that moment, it didn't matter how problematic the world was, is, and will always be.

It was just another Sunday.

Lesson Six:
You Are the Amalgamation
of Your Genealogy

Agbalagba Ju Julọ

They say that the mountain was a mystery.

Between her peaks and pockets of rock there were secrets. She went by many names: Mount Edlo, Tobacco Row, but back then she was called "Potato Hill." People say that once you'd go up that mountain, chances were, you weren't coming back down. There was magic in those hills. Old magic.

Napoleon Jefferson Eubanks and his son Jeff lived in a shack at the edge of the field on Howard Martin's farm. Day after day they worked on master's tobacco crops where the hot sun beat down on their backs. The only thing to shade his brow was a straw hat, one that always had a magpie feather tucked into the side. That feather, Napoleon swore, was a reminder of how his people once flew.

Napoleon would smoke out of his pipe made of clay and Jeff would read from the Bible his mother left him when he was born. Just before Napoleon would drift off to sleep, he'd always say to Jeff the same thing his father said to him: "You son, are a born fighter. I was named for a great man, and so are you."

On days when the harvest was high, Master sent Napoleon and Jeff to nearby farms to trade tobacco. Napoleon taught his son the ways of the mountain. How to track and trap animals. Which foot paths were safe. How to read the currents of the river. He also taught him the Tutelo tongue. Napoleon may have been a slave, but to Jeff he was king of that mountain. Not before long, the king passed down his crown.

Jeff grew up into a fine man. Never smoked like his daddy and tried chewing tobacco only once. He fell in love with a girl named Rose and together they jumped the broom. They had nine children that all grew up on the farm. Oh yes. Jeff was a fine man indeed, with as much of a happy life as a man could ask for.

But then, the War of the States began. There were rumors between the enslaved on the plantation that there were men in the hills, men who were fighting with other white folks like Master to set them free.

Winter was coming soon. Those men didn't know the lay of the land like the masters. Jeff knew he had to help. With harvest time around the corner, Master Martin would need him to do tobacco runs to nearby farms.

Rose packed her husband's mule as he kissed his children good-bye. He counted all their 180 fingers and toes. "One day," he told them, "you'll come up with me on this mountain. We are born fighters. I was named for a great man, and so are you." With that, he took his father's straw hat with the magpie feather, placed it on his head, tucked his Bible in his jacket pocket, and headed towards the mountain.

The first two days, Jeff tracked and trapped animals. He followed the foot paths and rivers his father taught him were safe and fished for trout. At night he'd sit by the fire and read from his Bible. When he was done, he'd tilt his father's hat over his face and stroke the feather until he fell asleep. On the third day on the mountain, Jeff figured he had trapped enough game to feed a small army. He knew he had enough tobacco left to keep the soldiers' minds at ease. And so, he set off, determined to do his part, and support their cause.

And those soldiers weren't too hard to find. Yankees had a habit of uprooting terrain so foreign under their heels. Jeff followed the heel tracks to a camp. There he found blue uniforms that hung on tree branches like leaves. Men of all ages sat around fires and washed in the river below.

"Good evenin, folks," Jeff called out to the men. The men scrambled looking for guns and weapons to defend themselves. "No, no. I ain't no enemy, sirs." Jeff took the sacks of meat hanging on his shoulder and threw it at the feet of a soldier.

The man took a step back and looked down. Once he grabbed his brimmed hat and saber, he motioned his arms to have the rest of the men ease their defense. "Well now," said the general, "looks like we have a sympathizer, lads! Tell me boy, what is your business here?"

"Well, I belong to a farmer down the mountain. Some of the other slaves said you all was up here. Said you were fighting to make us free. Thought I'd do my part to help you and brought you some supplies." Jeff reached into his mule's saddle bag and untied the stalks of tobacco. The general stroked his moustache. He looked over to the soldier behind him and nodded.

"Well, now. That's mighty kind of you. What did you say your name was?"

"Jeff, sir. Jeff Eubanks."

"Well, Jeff Eubanks, my name is Brigadier General Henry Abbott. And these here are my men. We're all very appreciative of your help."

Jeff replied, "Glad to give it, sir! Glad to give it! I can bring more supplies in two months' time, but next time I'll need some compensation so Master don' get suspicious."

The general nodded and held out his hand. "We'll see what we can do." Jeff smiled and shook the General's hand. He lifted his hat, tipped it, and mounted his mule. He went back down the mountain and back to the farm.

That night, around the glow of the fire, Jeff told his children tall tales about the soldiers in the mountain. When he was done, he took out his Bible and read the children the book of Exodus. And that night, all in the house dreamed of freedom.

Two months came and went. By now, Jeff had eleven children: Rose had twins. Master needed Jeff to run into the mountains to sell his tobacco before the first snowfall. And so, Jeff made out a plan to help both Master and the soldiers hidden on the mountain.

Jeff convinced Master to give him a cart and some oxen. Jeff reassured Master, he could get much more money if he had more supplies to sell.

Rose packed the ox-driven cart as he told his children goodbye. He counted all 220 fingers and toes. "One day," he told them, "y'all will come up with me on this mountain. We are born fighters. I was named for a great man, and so you." He kissed his wife and took his father's straw hat with the magpie feather, placed it on his head, tucked his Bible in his jacket pocket, and headed towards the mountain.

He drove straight to the soldiers' camp. Winter was coming soon, and there was no time to waste. In winter, Jeff knew that mountain was unforgiving. The men cheered as they saw Jeff and the oxen approaching. The general shook Jeff's hand and handed him a pouch of coins. "Thank you, Jeff," said General Abbott. "You truly are a lifesaver."

Lifesaver. Not a soul had ever called Jeff that, let alone a white man. Jeff tipped his hat and mounted his cart. "I'll be back in the Spring to check on you. Be seeing you, sir."

Jeff turned the cart around and left the camp. The next two days, Jeff tracked and trapped animals. He followed the foot paths his father taught him were safe. He cut down trees and stocked up firewood and filled the cart. When the cart was full of food and rations, he decided to head home.

As Jeff was finishing packing up his camp, he heard the sound of distant drums, jingling bells, and singing. Through the woods, he saw the Monacans' dancing around a fire. "Yipi: wo," the chief exclaimed, welcoming Jeff with a warm embrace. Together, Jeff and his friends sat and told stories around the fire. The next day, some tribal women gave Jeff a bearskin cloak. Winter is coming, the women warned. As they prayed over Jeff for his safe return, the chief gave him a jug of fire water for his travels. Jeff gave the chief some of his leftover tobacco. With the tip of his hat, he climbed the cart and continued to head home.

Halfway down the mountain, it started to snow.

Jeff worried about the oxen. With his mule, he could climb down safe and secure. But oxen were top-heavy and any slip could kill them all. Jeff found a nearby cave to take cover. For two days the snow continued. To pass the time, he'd sit by the fire and read from his Bible. When he was done, he'd tilt his father's hat over his face and stroke the feather until he fell asleep.

Days turned into weeks and the snow continued to fall. And Jeff continued to read and sleep. Between meals he'd drink the chief's fire water and drift back into sleep.

And sleep.

And sleep.

And sleep.

Jeff awoke to the sound of singing birds. He scratched his beard and hair, which felt a bit longer than he had remembered. The oxen were gone, but the cart remained. Outside the cave, green grass warmed his bare feet. Jeff figured he must've slept into spring.

He gathered what he could from the cart and made a knapsack for his back. By the time he got down the hill, unfamiliar Black bodies were off working the field. They stopped to stare at Jeff. Their clothes, while dirty, seemed well mended. They all wore shoes on their feet. That's odd, Jeff thought. Better not waste time. It was best to catch up with Master. Jeff knew his being away for so long was bound to stir up trouble. But first, he wanted to see his Rose and sweet children.

Jeff walked up to the small house where his shack once stood. Jeff knocked on the door, and a young Black girl answered. She looked the strange man up and down. Putting her hand on her hip she asked, "Who are you?"

Jeff was confused by the girl's question. Hadn't he only been gone a few months? Surely not long enough for anyone to forget his face. He responded, "Well, young lady, I happen to be Jeff Eubanks, and I used to live here. Do you happen to know where the family who used to live here went?"

The girl took a minute to think of an answer for the stranger's odd question. She looked behind her and then responded, "Well, sir, I'm ten. We've been living here as long as I've been alive. And my daddy lived here for a long time. And his daddy before that, and so on."

Jeff seemed puzzled by the answer. His daddy had built that shack. Jeff had grown up in that shack, and now it was gone as if it had never existed.

Jeff went to Master's house and knocked on the front door. A young man answered the door. He looked like Master—with the same brown hair and turned up nose—but his mouth seemed a little more crooked to the left.

"What do you want?"

"Is this Master Howard Martin's house?"

"Yes, this is him. I am Howard Martin the Third."

The Third? The boy rolled his eyes and slammed the door. Jeff was more confused than ever. He left the farm and headed towards town. In the middle of the square, Black people were celebrating. A banner waved high overhead where the word "Juneteenth" was painted against the sheet. Jeff grabbed the arm of a young woman dancing. "Excuse me ma'am," asked Jeff, "what is Juneteenth?"

The woman gave Jeff a quizzical look. "Why," she replied, "it's the day that we were set free." *Set free? Did this mean the soldiers had won?*

"Tell me, girl, what year is it? Did the soldiers win?"

"Why, it's 1950! And of course, we won! We showed the Axis of Evil a thing or two!" With that, the girl joined back to the festivities.

Jeff sank into himself with this news. 1950. He had slept for over 100 years. Slept through his marriage. Slept through watching his children grow. Slept through the sweet taste of freedom. He sat on a bench and began to cry. Between sobs he heard an announcer call the audience over.

"Okay y'all, time for the last event of the day, where we pay tribute to our ancestors and proclaim our Chieftain Elder. Who of you is king among us? Who has lived through greatness?"

Something told Jeff to raise his hand. As he did so, five other men did the same. The six men were ushered to the stage to stand before the crowd. One by one, they introduced themselves, Silas, Ezekiel, Harbo, Samuel, Theodore, and then Jeff. To prove their claims the town historian held the box of birth records and sat below the stage. As the men called out their names the crowd clapped as the historian would call out their ages. 79! 80! 87! 90! 93! By the time the historian got to Jeff, he couldn't find any record. As the historian shrugged his shoulders, the announcer approached Jeff. The announcer eyed Jeff up and down.

"Say sir, what happens to be your last name?"

"My name is Jeff. Jeff Eubanks. Son of Napoleon Eubanks."

The historian checked again and shrugged his shoulders.

"Do you have any proof of your age?" asked the announcer.

"No, sir." Jeff took off his hat and held it over his chest. "All I got is this here Bible that was given to me on the day of my birth from my mother. It is the most precious thing I own now."

Frustrated and alone, Jeff began to sob. The announcer took the Bible, handing it to the historian for a closer look. The historian whispered in the announcer's ear.

Upon hearing the remarks of the historian, the announcer exclaimed "136?! No. That can't be right. Check again."

The historian thumbed through the pages. In the crowd, an old woman screamed.

"Father! It is you!" She hobbled towards the stage as the crowd parted like the Red Sea before her path. The old woman took Jeff's face in between her palms and said, "I am Lily. Your youngest daughter. I was but an infant when you left. I remember your face as clear as day!"

He had found family at last, and not all was lost as he had so feared. The old woman introduced her father to her children, her grand-children, and their children. Jeff counted 1000 fingers and toes as one by one, all 50 of his remaining relatives introduced themselves by name. Jeff had never seen anything so glorious. That night, he learned the value of family and he swore to never leave them again. That night, there were two achievements celebrated in Lily's house-hold: the reunion of return and the preservation of ancestry. Long-lost relative Jeff Eubanks became Amherst County's Oldest Living Negro.

How to Dissect a Bleeding Heart

If you want to know what the human heart looks like, a dead sheep's heart is best for dissection. It also resembles the worst cut of a steak. The same beefy texture is thick and gray-brown matter devoid of blood. I learned this much today at the summer camp where I am a counselor. Staring at the dead organs in the pans, I watched as teenage girls in lab coats and rubber gloves prepared their specimens on the tables in front of them. The instructor of this training stood at the front of the room, with a heart in hand, and smiled at the students. "Are you ready?" He pulled his goggles over his glasses and flipped on the overhead projector. He grabbed a scalpel and set the heart down on the glass. "Okay, let's begin."

The morgue's pea-green walls remind me of baby vomit. How strange it is that a place of death like this smells like wet rubber cement. The attendant walks to the counter and lifts a blue fabric grocery bag onto the countertop. "Just need to see some ID, ma'am."

I hand him my driver's license and birth certificate. The man compares my credentials to the computer screen in front of him. His white mustache moves from side to side. He lowers his glasses to the bridge of his nose and coughs.

"I'm sorry. You're not listed as next of kin," he dryly asserts.

"I'm his daughter. He isn't married and he was homeless. There is no one else."

He hands me back the papers and my ID. "Says here only a Sherry Williams can have access to his things."

The man clearly doesn't care about the nuances of this situation. To him, it doesn't matter that I am standing here and claiming a man who never once claimed me. I am here for a father, no, a sperm donor, who happens to share my last name. This clerk doesn't want a sob story; this is another day at a job where paperwork leaves little room for empathy.

"Look. I have no idea who that is, but she isn't here and I am. Do you want to hold onto this stuff until she shows up, which she never will, or do you want to just get rid of it now?"

After a pause, the man nods and pulls out a form. "Sign here for release of Mr. Shelly Robert Hunter's personal effects."

I sign, grab the bag, and leave the morgue. When I get to my car, I fling the bag in the passenger seat.

Twenty-five years. Twenty-five years I have not seen this man. He has to die for me to have him. The noon sun shines on the bag as if I am supposed to open it. As if, by opening it, I can peek inside the very ethos of my father and what was supposed to be.

In this one small blue bag I see my own mortality. In the end everything we are, we own, and cherish can be reduced to a little blue bag. Five pairs of underwear, one blue navy shirt, one red buttoned Hawaiian shirt with faded seafoam-green palm trees, a watch, ten dollars in quarters, a silver ring with etchings of a bear, one lottery card, a key, a receipt for a $144.85 cash withdrawal, a packet of saltine crackers. I dig through the bag to find the missing piece of this narrative.

My fingers catch on some string. I pull my hand out to find a pink digital camera. My stomach tightens. *This is it. I have found him.*

The last picture I had of my father was the two of us at the Grand Canyon. In our matching teal outfits, he holds me high over the mountainous landscape. He looks at me lovingly, a three-year-old version of me waves at my mother taking the photo. His face, his hands tell the lens: *This is my child.*

That would be the last time I ever saw my father. He would instead become gaps of memory where memories of him were supposed to go, spaces I'd try to fill when I'd close my eyes and picture him. Try to remember his height. The sound of his voice. The texture of his salt-and-pepper beard.

As a child, I remember watching *A Little Princess*. My favorite part of the movie was when the little girl finds her father and he doesn't remember her because of a head injury. As she's being taken away, she screams and somehow, as if by chance, the father remembers. He runs up to her in the rain and cradles her. He whispers, "I'm sorry."

A fatherless child then dreamed that she too would find her father.

I turn on the screen and hit "display."

The first picture is of the moon, the same moon I had taken pictures of a thousand times. The next is of my father in a hospital bed hooked up to machines, waving to the camera. In another, a woman is laying on the bed with him and they kiss. Maybe this was *Sherry.* In another, they are in a restaurant, him smiling, her coyly hiding her face. I scoff and scroll to the next, but then my stomach squeezes again at the sight: a picture of the couple outside of the restaurant. I recognize where he is: a good fifty feet from my house. Fifty feet away and he didn't even bother to know me or find me.

I throw the camera onto the back seat. My breathing deepens. Tears pool in the corners of my eyes like a slow, advancing flood. A knot begins to form in my skull. It pounds against the cranial lining from the inside out. Twenty-five years. Fifty feet. Seventy-five ways to be a dad and my father chose none of them.

I pick up the last remaining item in the bag, my father's wallet. In the center fold, one-hundred dollars sat. Figuring I'm owed for all the missed birthdays, I stick the money inside my breast pocket. I thumb past the ID cards, the Costco and EBT cards stuffed inside, until something falls out and into my lap. A bright blue Durex condom. Immediately I think of my half-siblings, all girls with all different last names. I think about how my father used cocaine and refused to work up until the day he died. Working odd landscaping and home-repair gigs bankrolled his addiction. I think about all the women who will mourn him, and all I can do is laugh.

"The heart," the instructor says, "is the perfect engine. With two lobes full of tissue and muscle, it pumps the backflow of blood."

Once the girls identify the outer anatomy of the heart, they are told to look for the "T," the anterior interventricular morticular. When a big blockage beginning in the left main artery or the left anterior of the descending artery creates a heart attack, the site of this blockage is called the widow-maker. Prior to modern medical treatments the widow-maker was a fast and quick way to die.

With precision, the girls take their scalpels and slice through the heart carefully to create an incision halfway through. The heart's tough exterior proves difficult for some as they look to me with pleading eyes. As a counselor, I cannot do this for them. I instead try to guide their small and delicate hands.

"His fat ass won't fit," I text my mom an hour before the funeral service, with a picture of my father's cremains awkwardly stuffed into a large mosaic candy dish I purchased at TJ Maxx. After funeral costs and cremation services, there wasn't much money left. My father's bank account had about $200 and between the morgue, finding a low-cost funeral director, and a church to host the service, I am stretched thin.

"Dad says you can borrow his humidor," Mom responds. "Once you get here, he'll give it to you, and then we can head to the church."

My stepfather wanted to adopt me when I was ten. He sat me down, asked me to take his last name, and call him Dad. I agreed to call him Dad, but I still held out hope for my father to return. Perhaps he wouldn't love me if I was no longer a Hunter. Perhaps that would make it harder for my father to find me. Boy, how I was wrong.

At my parents' house, my Dad sits at his computer.

"This is a nice thing you're doing for him," Dad says as he hands me the humidor. "I'm proud of you."

"Thanks," I reply, placing my father inside the large wooden box.

"Don't lose it," Dad scolds in the way dads like to do. "I like my Cubans almost as much as I like you," he teases.

Mom and I drive to the church in the Hill District. There are parts of this city that still feel estranged. In the ways that Homestead was my mother's childhood home, the Hill was my father's.

Outside the church in the parking lot, my sister Simone stands next to her mother and holds my nine-month-old niece, Olivia. My four-year-old nephew, Omari, plays with tiny pebbles and lines them up, counting each one. We hug each other and step inside the church to prepare for the service. I place the humidor in front of the altar, and we all sit down in a pew, my mother (my father's first wife), me, Simone, and at the end, her mother Sylvia (my father's high school sweetheart). It's like the start of a bad joke. A woman with over-dyed red hair mixed with limp gray walks up to us as if to deliver the punchline.

"I'm so sorry for your loss," she says to my mother.

"Thank you," my mother smiles.

She tries to touch my hand. "Thank you for doing this for my Shelly."

Her Shelly?

"It's been so tough with him gone. My children really miss him." Next to me, Olivia starts to stir as Simone bounces her on her chest and tries to console her.

This woman, Cynthia, I am told, continues, "He was the love of my life, and I am just so distraught."

Sylvia rolls her eyes and Simone's knee nudges mine. My mother's smile fades, and she dryly responds, "I'm so sorry for *your* loss."

A man walks up behind her and ushers her toward the other side of the church pews. Before she sits, she pulls a picture frame with my father's picture and a peace sign sticker on it and places it next to the humidor. She kisses the box and buckles at the altar. The same man grabs her shoulders, whispers into her ear, and forces her to sit down.

As people trickle into the church, they walk up to us and introduce themselves. These are my father's friends. His classmates. His network that neither Simone nor we are privy to. They offer their condolences, and we thank them even if we don't need condolences to mourn a nonfather. The reverend begins and we sing "Amazing Grace."

He offers a sermon and tells us that Shelly is now with the angels and his mother. When the sermon is complete, he asks me to deliver the eulogy.

How do you pay tribute to a man you never knew? How do you mourn when you're only tethered by blood and by name? Prior to this moment, I was proud that I wasn't a bastard. My parents had been married and I was the result of their love. A love where my father sent my mother flowers every year for her birthday up until he died.

Before the cancer riddled his body, my father had wanted to meet me.

Apparently, he had heard that I was writing a book for my master's. Days before we were finally going to meet, he died. My mother apologetically told me so over the phone.

I wrote a poem about my father. If I'm honest, I don't think it was any good. My heart wasn't in it. When they know you're a writer, there's an expectation of eloquence. As I read, the audience sits engaged. I want to show them that, despite my father's absence, my mother raised me right. You pay tribute to your elders and forgive their transgressions—at least, that's what I was taught. That poem, that sorry-ass excuse for creative writing, would be the last one I'd write for years to follow.

One by one people are encouraged to speak about my father. Each story speaks of wondrous memories. But I can't help but notice my sister's rocking of her child becoming more ferocious. The thumps of her back vibrate through the church pew. As Cynthia stands to say a few words, the rocking only gets worse.

"Shelly was the love of my life for thirty years…"

Thirty years? I do the math in my head. I am twenty-eight. Simone is thirty-four. We have one sister who is a few months older than me and another that is older than Simone. Despite our best efforts, no one could find them.

Cynthia continues, "Even though he wasn't theirs biologically, my children always called him Dad—"

Simone's rocking grows to a near-violent thrashing. The wood squeaks as Olivia's infantile wails become inconsolable.

In her lavender jumpsuit and matching heels, my mother could not look more beautiful to me at this moment. In lilac purple cat-eyed frames, neither my mother's eyes nor eyebrows flinch. She sighs, checks her watch, pulls out some mints and offers me one. Her stone cold, business-as-usual demeanor exudes grace as Cynthia's erratic behavior appalls. It is glorious.

Sylvia mutters something under her breath and continues to roll her eyes.

Am I dreaming this? Is this chick serious?

Cynthia again buckles under the weight of her words. She flings herself over the humidor and wails. Her tears begin to drench the wood. A man tries to console her and usher her to take her seat. In a final outburst, Cynthia tries to take the humidor. The reverend takes the box from her and places it back upon the altar.

"Is there anyone else who would like to say a few words?"

A raspy voice comes from the back of the church. "I got soomm-mmeeethhinnn to say!"

An ashy, old Black man hobbles up the aisle. As he reaches the podium, he sets a brown paper bag on top. He looks at his captivated audience and smiles, revealing a silver-capped front tooth that off-sets the remaining yellow ones. He clears his throat.

"I went to high school with Shelly. And the whole time all the girls would always chase him around. Never could figure out why. Now as I'm standing here, I can understand it. Looking at his two beautiful daughters, I can see that Shelly could make some pretty-ass babies."

My mother and Sylvia's mouths hang wide open. Simone stands up in disbelief as Olivia wails in her arms. The man smiles, takes a swig from his bag, and bows. In this moment, I decide that I hate Black funerals. Every movie, every Tyler Perry play, could not prepare me enough for this level of dysfunction.

The girls pull apart the heart strings. One by one, they count the pieces of dried, fleshy muscle. They follow along with the mapping of the heart and identify the aortas. The branch and the apex. With little flag pins, they identify the valves, the extracellular matrices. They learn terms like "morphogenesis," where the heart has the capability to change, to grow.

When the dissection is done, the instructor tells the girls that now we must stitch the heart back together. I assist by helping to pass out kits of needles and threads. We must suture what damage we have caused.

Tequila is Simone and Brittany's liquor of choice. Together we take shots next to our father's cremains and pour one out for his ghost. Overhead, music blares out of the speaker at this Mexican restaurant, Señor Frog's, sandwiched between a McDonald's and an auto dealership in Dormont.

Brittany is the only other legitimate sister. She was the product of our father's second marriage. Simone had managed to find her through Facebook.

Together, we take turns joking about the ways in which our father was a deadbeat. "At least y'all had his last name," Simone jokes.

I pour another shot, shoot it back, and bite the lime.

"Perhaps it was divine intervention that our father only had daughters."

As the shots of tequila saturate my stomach, I think about how, growing up as an only child, I dreamed of having siblings. That night, my childhood wishes on stars and held out hopes came to fruition. In this tiny Mexican restaurant in the middle of nowhere, Shelly had proved that he did one something right: us.

We were the remnants of what made him so great. Years later, Simone and I would go on a backpacking trip in Europe together. We would call each other on birthdays, and I'd cheer for every milestone that Olivia and Omari would achieve. In the end, I found our father and my long-lost search had been answered. In my sisters, the open hole my father had created could be filled.

Lesson Seven:
You are Stardust Reimagined:
Dream for the Cosmos

WA OMỌ RẸ

You know what that ol' African proverb says: *Dreams are related to the past, but they are also connected to the future.*

In this dream, Charlie was a magpie. A beautiful bird of onyx and ivory feathers perched high in a tree, she looked over the hills of Homestead. Around her, the air became clouded with thick, black, suffocating smoke. She tried to use her wings to wave it away from her face, but the more she waved, the more the smoke stuck to her feathers. There was nothing left to do but fly.

She leaped from her nest and winged to new heights. Pittsburgh became nothing more than smoke and land. Before long, the land below her turned into water. Water stretched far beyond what her eyes could see. She could smell the salt wafting into her beak and the sun felt warm on her back.

But then, the sun disappeared. A storm began to brew along the horizon. Whirling winds and the crashes of thunder and rain made her feathers feel heavy, made her wings wobble and strain to fly straight.

And then, a cloud opened its mouth and swallowed her whole. When she awoke, she found herself in the arms of a woman with conch shells for earrings who smelled of ginger and allspice. The woman fed her fish. She whispered, "You have made your way home. I have missed you."

Charlie loved Pittsburgh, but there was a part of her that dreamed of flying off to new lands. Her arms felt homesick for something more. And so, she decided to travel to find it.

Ghana was nothing like Charlie had seen. The red clay roads, the pregnant baobab trees, and the dust-colored cattle felt strange yet familiar. The way that women sang over wash tubs and hung their gonja cloths over clotheslines reminded her of her own mother and aunties singing in their shared laundry rooms. Over fufu and salted fish, she laughed with new friends. She sat between thighs as women braided her hair with beads.

Months went by and Charlie flowered. One day at the market, while she was buying new kente cloth, a woman called her from a nearby tent.

"Hey, girl. Yes, you. Come. I have been waiting for you."

Charlie put down the cloth and followed the woman.

"Sit," the woman ordered. "Let me tell you your fortune."

The woman smelled of ginger and allspice, like her dream. *Could this be her?*

Charlie sat on the stool in front of the woman. Gray dreadlocks beaded with shells peeked through her golden headwrap. As she reached for Charlie's hand, she smiled.

"You have made your way home to us, I see," the old woman began.

"Well, I'm not from here, actually. I've just been living here for a bit," Charlie responded.

"Yes, but your soul is from here, child. It flew from here long ago. I have dreamed of you." The woman spread Charlie's palm wide and traced the lines with her finger. She poured some cashew nuts into her hand and closed it. "Throw," the old woman ordered, pointing to the ground.

Charlie did as she was told and threw the nuts onto the mat. The old woman studied the nuts, counting each one in a diagonal pattern. "Ah. This is good. Very good. Just like my dream. And in this dream, I dreamt of fish."

"Really?" Charlie asked. "Will I be successful and make a lot of money?"

"No," the woman replied. "But your child will take care of you, and you will be great through them."

Child? Charlie was still so young. She didn't have time to be having no babies. At least, not yet.

"Take this egg," the woman instructed. "When you fly back home, bury this in the ground and be sure to sit on it for three days. If the yolk turns red, then you'll know it worked."

The woman shoved a chicken egg into Charlie's hand and pushed her out of the tent. Charlie went to go back in but as she lifted the tent flap, the old woman had already disappeared.

That night, Charlie decided that her time in Africa should come to a close. She missed her family and her Pittsburgh home.

Years passed, and Charlie stayed in Pittsburgh. She found love, got a degree from a local school, and grew up. The egg, Charlie decided, was too precious to throw away. It was her only proof that the old woman had existed.

But after a few years, it started to smell.

"Throw that stinking thing away," her husband pleaded.

Her husband, well intentioned though he was, didn't understand. This egg, Charlie knew, felt important. Instead, she decided the best thing to do was to bury it. That way, she always knew where it was and could keep it safe.

After she finished burying the egg, Charlie sat and read a book. Before long, night came, and she fell asleep on the grass. That night, she dreamed of fish.

Something told Charlie that she needed to stay, needed to protect the egg in case anyone was to discover it. Before long, two days had passed. On the third day, she discovered that a mole had dug a hole way too close to where the egg rested. *Oh no!* Charlie thought, frantically digging at the ground.

Thankfully, she found that the egg remained intact.

There was only one difference: a tiny crack where a little green sprout began to grow. Had she buried the egg next to a root? Did the old woman's advice work? Charlie cracked the egg to see where the sprout came from. Out of it poured a crimson-red yolk where, attached to the root of the sprout, a baby the size of a bean stared at Charlie and started to cry.

That was the day that Charlie became a mother. Charlie learned to never question dreams, fortunes, nor their elder tellers. The youth may walk faster, but the elders know the way.

I Am

There is power in the tongue.
Pushed against half-closed lips,
its intent is to breathe truth
into thin air.
"Truth is important," my father says.
It hurts, but you have to be honest.
Honesty,
is pure.
Be pure.

In West Africa, the childbirth naming ceremony typically takes place seven to ten days after the baby is born. The elders have to make sure that the baby intends to stay among the living. A name is a bond between body and soul. Without one, a being has no driven purpose. The elders wait until a story can be told, and only then can a child be labeled.

In Alex Haley's *Roots,* Kunte Kinte holds his newborn child in his arms. "Your name is your shield," he tells her. "And I will name you

Kizzy which means *stay put*, but not *stay slave*. Kizzy, you are the daughter of Kunte Kinte and Belle, and though you will never know them, the granddaughter of Omoro and Binta Kinte." He holds the child towards the night sky and exclaims, "Behold! The only thing greater than you!"

While many of us have lost our native tongues, we still know the importance that a name will bring. Our ancestors' bodies were carried here against their will. They were given new names too foreign to bear any true meaning that never stuck. Their traditions remained on the tip of their tongues.

My mother knew of the power in a name.

I was born in a time when Black people were giving their children African names. Even still, my mother named me after a white woman. My mother, the woman who had lived in Ghana and cultivated her own personal collection of African antiquities, chose to brandish me with a tool that could commit guerilla warfare in the job market. She claims that she wanted to "give me a chance." What she really means is that she didn't want the world to dismiss another Black child. She knew even then that a name is the world's first impression of you. She loved Dylan Thomas' poems. Loved the rhythm and its depth. When she saw his wife—Caitlin—was a writer too, her mind was made up. Little did she know in the 1980s a gross majority of pregnant white women had liked the name, too.

I met my first Kaitlin in 6th grade. She was blonde, tall, with green eyes, and loved Limp Bizkit. Our July birthdays were two days apart. Because her last name ended in a J and mine an H we always sat together in every class. I thought that we would be best friends. But then her and Favia—the only other Black girl in class—started to become friends. Kaitlin started calling herself "Spigot." Even gave Favia a nickname like "Sparky." Favia had done me no wrong and yet she became my bitter rival. I wanted a cool nickname, too. A pre-teen like me wanted to belong.

By the time our twelfth birthdays rolled around, I tried one last time to be Kaitlin's friend.

My parents threw me a party with a waterslide and a barbeque. I invited all the girls from class—Kaitlin and Favia included. We danced to N*SYNC and Backstreet Boys. Sitting in a circle, we played games and giggled, high from ice cream cake and soda. Everything seemed to be going just fine. I sat in triumph that my party had worked until my mom decided to be the party's buzzkill.

"Why Spigot?" my mother asked while washing dishes.

"Huh?" Kaitlin asked, stuffing more Cheeto puffs into her mouth.

"Oh. Where does your nickname come from? It's a common term from Pittsburgh, so I was just curious."

Despite my mother's innocent and honest question, my pre-teen addled brain registered nothing but embarrassment. Adults are to be seen and not heard at parties. Mortified, I scowled at my mother. I looked at Kaitlin with apologetic eyes. *Please don't ruin this, Mom.* Kaitlin smirked and continued eating.

"Just thought it sounded cool, I guess."

She seemed so cool. Completely unfazed by anything. Soon after, the party ended. I said goodbye to Kaitlin and thanked her for coming. I think I even awkwardly hugged her. Despite my mother's embarrassing comment, a part of me assumed that we were cool. Until I found out I was the only girl not invited to her birthday party. My childhood friend, Brenna, told me there was a rumor floating around that I was a lesbian.

Apparently, word got out that I made out with a girl during a sleepover.

"No one wanted to hang out with a homosexual," Brenna told me. "I don't care what you are. We go way back."

Homosexual? I didn't know many people outside of my godfather and my mother's friends who were lesbians or gay. I didn't *feel* like I was one. I didn't know that some people can be attracted to both men and women. Didn't know it was okay. The spectrum of sexuality and orientation for middle school children like us did not exist in 2000. Again, someone had tried to name me. Out me as something I didn't see myself as being. Shortly after that summer, I dropped out of honors classes entirely. It was easier to make myself small.

The next year in school, many kids started to call me a new name: Oreo. Perhaps it was the only way to explain away a Black girl who rocked a Sex Pistol shirt, sharpie-colored Chuck Taylors, and Princess Leia buns. Instead, I started hanging out with non-white kids. I hung out with Twinkies, Coconuts, and the assortment collection of Others measured against the backdrop of a brown paper bag. It was easier to fit in where we didn't belong.

Before we met and became high school sweethearts, in 8th grade, I remember talking to Mike on a three-way call. No matter how much my friend Krystal and I swore that I was Black, and she was

Filipino, he wouldn't believe it. To him, my voice and my name were a ventriloquist's trick.

"After all," he replied, "your name is *Caitlyn.*"

And there it was. A subliminal message embedded between the two syllables: Cait: NOT lyn: WHITE. It wasn't that Caitlyn was a unique name, it was uniquely not Black. From that time going forward I'd be saved in cell phones and remembered as "Black Caitlyn" as if to tell me apart from the regular (white) ones.

I had one goal senior year: to be on every single page of the yearbook. I joined Choir, Theatre/Junior Thespians, Lacrosse the year before, Model UN, French club, Media Aides, Book Club, you name it. That spring, I eagerly scanned through every name in my senior yearbook. Out of roughly 1,000 students there were only five Caitlyns. None of us spelled ours the same. In fact, on every page where I was featured, *my* name was never spelled the same.

To be both Black and a Caitlyn slowly became a crux. For a long time, I've grappled with what Black is and what Black isn't. I've danced between this binarized strata where my textured hair signified Blackness, but loving Star Wars or anime put me in spaces reserved for whiteness. With a name like Caitlyn, I spent a lifetime defending and demonstrating that the color of my skin could co-exist with the things that made me, me.

By the time I got to college, another white Caitlin from Minnesota lived across the hall from my dorm room, and I didn't even bother to differentiate. I was tired. Just plain tired. I went by Cait instead and kept it pushing.

"Why couldn't you have named me Shaniqua?" I ask my mother constantly.

"I didn't want you to be tagged," my mother constantly apologizes.

"But you could've named me Brittany or Ashley or literally anything else!"

"I wanted to give you anonymity."

According to the *Freakonomics* podcast, "Caitlin" ranked #14 on the list of the 20 "whitest" girl names. Certain names, like derivatives of Katherine, are statistically more likely to be chosen by parents who have a higher degree of education. The implication, Steven Levitt and Stephen Dubner state, is that Black-sounding names carry an "economic penalty." A study they mention found that if you send out a resume with a white-sounding name, it's about 50 percent more likely to get a callback than an identical resume with a Black-sounding name. A name, in this context, is an indicator of privilege from the cradle to the grave.

But it's their conclusion that moves me. It explains my mother's motives perfectly: parents use names to really impose their own expectations for their children's future success. In this vein, my mother gave me a shield. In name, she expected that I would "pass." Perhaps, in some ways, I have.

In my second year of grad school, I took a Creative Nonfiction workshop. I wrote an essay about my name. Vignette by vignette, I tried to outline glimpses of memories. I wrote about being stopped by police; about how my friend Taneesha couldn't find a job because of her name. I wrote about watching TV with my mom when Caitlyn Jenner announced to the world her new name. I ignorantly wrote about the times when people would ask me how to spell mine as I would deadname: "like Bruce." I wrote about the disheartening feeling when I Googled my name and found out that a white woman from North Carolina used it as a pseudonym to write Native American romance novels.

None of these snippets were discussed in the workshop that day.

Nothing about these moments resonated as having any real significance for my professor or classmates. The only thing a classmate unabashedly felt was important to comment on was that my writing didn't seem "Black enough." The term "inauthentic" swirled around the room. The phrase, "I want to understand what it means to be Black here," was unapologetically requested.

I—the only Black person—was told just to sit there and take their criticisms. It was the classroom policy to just say "thank you."

No one ever questions what it means to feel white. No one wants to know that translation. In that classroom I was put on display. I was expected to perform. I was expected to Blacksplain and simultaneously support their bias. That classroom wanted to feel validated for their stereotypical assumptions of what Black was. That moment was the day I devised my first question: well, what does it *mean* to be Black anyways?

One time, I met another Black Kaitlin. She was lighter than me, with curly hair that perfectly bounced and laid flat, and she was getting her master's degree in Spanish. As she laughed off the coincidence in our names, I was resolved to hate her. I could only fixate on the idea that her presence had somehow stolen the one thing that made me unique. Here we both were at a dinner table—with *our* white friends—and yet, there were two Black Caitlyns. I had made up my mind that there could only be one. I refused to be Black Caitlyn #2.

Of course, she had done me no wrong. Her mother, like mine, had found something meaningful in the name. Loved the way it sounded and looked on a page. But in that moment, none of that mattered. She defied the one self-deprecating joke I had:

Know how you won't forget my name?

Think of the whitest name possible for a Black girl.

I'm the only one you'll ever meet.

Her presence ruined the punchline. She was whiter, sounded whiter, and had that *good* hair like a white girl. No matter how many times we are taught to never judge a book by its cover, that doesn't really matter when you're Black. We read each other because we are conditioned to do so. We pit ourselves against one another and judge based on our proximity to whiteness. And so, instead of getting to know this girl better and find common solidarity in a name, I preferred to silently scowl at her from across the room for two hours.

Why must we compromise ourselves and hush the whispers of our very sense of self because of a name? What good does it do anyone to make ourselves small and confined to fit the structure that institutions of whiteness created?

My mother got a DNA Ancestry test. She says she wanted to learn more about where she comes from. What she really means is that she has lost her way and is trying to rebind herself from an ancestral tether. She means to demonstrate to me that Black is not a monolith.

When my mother showed me the results, they claim that she is 68% African and 31% European. Of that 68%, half is Nigerian, 17% Benin, and 13% Bantu. I think about this amalgamation, try to find its meaning compared to how my white boyfriend can trace his lineage back to the settlement outside of Pittsburgh on his mother's side, and a small Greek village on his father's. My mother cannot trace her ancestry any further than the farm in which my great-great-grandmother was emancipated—the plantation my great-grandfather flew North from only to roost in Pittsburgh and spend the next 60 years slaving away in a steel mill—the same steel mill where my grandfather spent 40 years of his life after his father's retirement.

But despite what is missing, there is beauty in my mother's DNA results. It tells me that we came from great tribes. We came from the great Minon warriors of former Dahomey.

We, like our mothers before us, rocked bantu knots in our hair and migrated, flying great distances within Mother Africa before white slavers clipped our wings. Most of all, in spite of a system designed to eradicate our humanity, we persevered. We continue to thrive.

We are so great that we can name ourselves as anything.

I too, come from this greatness.

My mother named me Caitlyn because she wanted me to be a

warrior. She wanted my name to uplift me so I can float between spheres. In doing so, she made me a spectral anomaly and for that I am thankful. My name, Caitlyn, means *pure* and I am. Purely Black, and unapologetically.

I am everything I am supposed to be. I am a coalescence of those who came before me and will come after me and I find peace in that—even if I have a white girl name.

At the dispensary, I hand the clerk my patient ID. He looks at the name and looks back at me.

"You're not going to believe this, girl," he smiles, handing back my card.

I'm intrigued. "Oh?"

"I kid you not, my childhood best friend has the exact same name as you."

Here we go. Another white Caitlyn. I feign surprise.

"Oh wow. That's unreal!"

He hands me his phone.

"Yeah, girl. She has the most beautiful voice. You gotta see it."

And he was right. I look on the phone and a beautiful dark-skinned Black woman with glasses stares back smiles with a septum piercing and teal gauged ears. Her handle is perfect: Kai, Asshole with a heart of gold.

I follow her on Instagram. She DMs me: *Are we secretly related? Lmao.*

We text back and forth.

My Daddy is from the Hill; her daddy is from the East.

We conclude that we aren't in fact related.

I respond: *Imma still adopt you as a cuzzo. At the very least another Black Caitlyn (Kaitlin sp?) is fam in my opinion. We're rare.*

She responds: *A fact lol.*

It doesn't matter if we're blood. Our names forever make us soulbound.

The fact that Black Caitlyns thrive and survive in spite of our white names is enough for me.

There's a Black writer whose name is Kaitlyn Greenidge. Her book *Libertie* seems interesting. Part of me wants to send her a message. Ask her about her experiences and if she's ever written about *her* name. Instead, I pre-order the book. I resign myself to get to know her the way I want others to know me: through the composition of my words.

Lesson Eight:
Listen to Whispers and Allow Them to Guide You

Gbọ Fun Awọn Iwin

Once upon a time, there was a little girl named Carole who folks round the way called Lil Skippy Bird. Everyone said that Lil Skippy Bird was special. Always whispering to shadows and giggling to herself. Knew things that couldn't be described or explained away. Little did they know that Lil Skippy Bird had *the sight*.

And her story goes like this:

The matriarch of the family died, and it left a gaping wound in their hearts. Looking into the casket at her viewing on tippy toes, Skippy Bird waved at her grandmother's lifeless body and whispered into her ear, "I'll be seeing you later." Everybody thought it was strange. Nobody dared to ask questions. You never ask questions when you want to avoid the answers and it's even more impolite to gossip at funerals.

Nellie Cole's body had been in the ground for two days. Skippy Bird loved to play with dolls. Hour after hour she'd sit and talk and laugh just carrying on upstairs. Her mother and her Auntie were downstairs having tea when the ruckus upstairs became too much for their ears. When ordered to come down and asked what she was doing, Skippy Bird replied with a shrug and said, "I'm just playing with Grandma."

Things only became stranger after that.

As Skippy Bird grew, she would talk about dreams. Dreams where Grandma Nellie gave her recipes or numbers for her mother and father to play. She always knew where money was hidden in walls. Always knew things before they were about to happen.

People said that it was a guardian angel, but Skippy Bird knew better. The ancestors did, too. Used her as a conduit to help the family thrive and as an exchange, they watched over her, too. After her Uncle Silas died, he visited her bedside.

Skippy Bird got real sick one day. No doctors could find answers for her ailment. No matter what concoctions her mother tried, her fever only got worse. Each night, Uncle Silas stood at the foot of Skippy Bird's bed and watched over her attentively like a soldier. He'd grin and sing to his niece and she'd sleep as his ghostly palms touched her forehead. People say one night her fever caught a chill, and the fever dwindled shortly thereafter.

Uncle Silas followed Skippy Bird everywhere she went. And every night, he'd stand at her bedside and grin. Every night, he'd place his ghostly hand on her forehead and guard her while she slept.

Skippy Bird grew up into a fine woman. She was strong, smart, and a hard worker. She eventually moved away from her Pittsburgh home, but Uncle Silas followed, never far behind. And every night, he'd stand by her bedside and grin. Every night, he'd place his ghostly hand on her forehead, and guard her while she slept.

One day Skippy Bird met a handsome man at a party. While all the women swooned and swayed over him, he only had eyes for her. When Skippy Bird finally allowed for the man to take her on a date, he couldn't be more beside himself. He took her to a fancy restaurant and over music, they danced, and he sang in her ear.

The night of Skippy Bird's wedding, the two lovers laid in bed together as she told her new husband about her gift. Just as she was about to introduce her beau to her Uncle Silas, she saw that the ghost was no longer there.

And he hasn't come back ever since.

Passing the Torch

She tells me the story of each picture in her photo albums: her trip to Atlantic City with Uncle George, a picture from the *Pittsburgh Courier* where she and a bunch of girls visited the VA during World War II to write love letters to soldiers overseas and boost morale. With each turn of the page, there is a story. So many to hold onto that all I can do is take it in and hit "record" on my phone.

My favorite photo is of her in her twenties, freshly divorced with a red dress that ties around her neck. "Ooh, your Uncle George hated this one," my Aunt Bert chuckles. She takes the photo out of the album and walks over to her closet. "This one needs to go in with my collection." After a moment of rifling, she beckons me to join her at the closet door.

"Here is the suit I want to be buried in." She unzips a plastic floral bag hanging in the closet. It's a pearly pink two-piece dress suit fit for Jackie Onassis herself. She shows me the pumps, and the bag of underwear, too. She takes the picture, puts it into a bag with some others. "These," she exclaims, "are the photos I want in my obituary and this," she hands me a piece of notebook paper, "is the poem I wrote."

Two stanzas and eight lines: the rhyme pattern seems obvious. But these are her words, and my experience as a writing professor has trained me to encourage the process and applaud the courage that self-expression takes. "I had no idea you wrote, Aunt Bert," I say, handing back the poem.

"You thought you were the *only* writer in this family, girl?" She retorts. "Shoot, you got that talent from somewhere. Same as your cookin."

On her perfectly made bed, we lay out all her albums. On our stomachs, she points to my great-grandparents, my grandfather and grandmother, my mother, me. There are nine decades of photographs held between my fingertips.

"You know I used to sit here and cry when I'd look at these photos. But now all I remember are the good times and how I'll see these people soon." She encourages me to take these photos. "No one wants them," she claims, shoving dozens into my hands with attached post-it notes outlining who, and what, and where.

Before I leave, I kiss her and tell her I love her. "I'll be back sometime next week," I half-heartedly promise. "Don't forget that cobbler, girl! And pull out one of those crab cakes out from the freezer on your way out. I'm fixing to have a feast tonight." Aunt Bert changes the channel to the news from in her bedroom. I pull out the crab cakes that I made her from the freezer. I pull the tub of peach-blueberry cobbler from my bag and leave it on the kitchen counter. I write a little sticky note and leave it on the lid:

I love you. Enjoy. ☺

Two days later, I get a call from my mother while I'm at my boy-friend's parents' house for dinner. From her nasally tone and sniffs I can tell that she is upset. I excuse myself and go outside. Aunt Bert has died of a heart attack.

Days before the funeral, me, my boyfriend, my cousins, and my Aunt Carole start to clean out Aunt Bert's apartment. Over Beyoncé and Aretha, we dance and laugh and reminisce, and the tears and the pain weave in between. We find jars and envelopes of money stashed in cabinets and in sock drawers. There are old record albums and record players in fine and pristine condition sandwiched be-tween VCR Tapes. It's a treasure trove of odd antiquities and mem-ories.

We find more photographs. Ones we've never seen, and Aunt Bert probably didn't know she had. We stack them high and pile them into a box and try to figure out what to do with them. Carlton, my mother's first cousin, bundles them up and puts them into my hand. "Cait, you're the keeper of our stories now."

After that night and the days following my Aunt Bert's funeral, I've wondered about the stories I never knew, and the stories I've yet to find. How many Black stories have never been told? What is lost when we don't speak truth into every story every time that we tell it? Do we become haunted by the ghosts of our generational traumas if we choose not to listen to these whispers?

Before she died, my Aunt Bert said that her little brother Joe came to visit her often. She called him her guardian angel. He died from a ruptured appendix and was buried on her tenth birthday. From that day on, he visited her in dreams. He always said that "if you will live your life the way Momma taught you how to live, nothing bad will ever happen to you."

I wonder what things Aunt Bert will whisper into my ear as I dream.

I wonder how our stories will continue to grow.

Acknowledgements

I would like extend my deepest gratitude to my editor Risa and copy-editor Heather, whose care and attention to detail (and patience with me on deadlines) has made this book the treasure that it is now.

To my love and partner Nick, I am beyond thankful for the kindness that you show me daily. Thank you for bingeing anime and RuPaul's Drag Race on days when I need to recalibrate. Thank you for reminding me to eat and being the best dog dad ever. I love the life we have together, and I love you dearly, best friend.

To my parents, thank you for always believing in me even at times when I didn't believe in myself. Your guidance, patience, humor, and encouragement are what make me the person I am today. I would be nothing without you. Everything I do is to make you proud.

To my Aunt Carole, Uncle Booker, Uncle Archie, and the extended Coles family, thank you for your stories, your love, and your support. A huge thank you to my cousin Carly for taking my inspiration to heart and creating such a beautiful book cover. To my cousins old and young and far and near, I want you to know there are way too many names to list you individually, but I will say that I love you all immensely. While these may be my words, this book belongs to you.

To my godparents Aunt Karen and Uncle Ken: thank you for being my day ones. Thank you for being there through every memory and loving me unapologetically and enthusiastically. I love you beyond words.

To my professors Kathy Glass, Emad Mirmomatahari, Linda Kinnahan, Danielle St. Hilaire, and the other esteemed faculty at Duquesne University: thank you for always nurturing my pursuits and for your constant encouragement. Your mentorship has been tremendous.

To the professors at Chatham University, thank you for your support and guidance. Sheila Squillante you are and will forever be a tremendous mentor and a guiding star.

To my undergraduate professors Bill Beverly, Wendy Bilen, Lori Shpunt, Liza Child and the Trinity Washington community, thank you for taking a little seedling like me and giving me the tools to thrive and grow.

To my darling sister Simone, my beautiful niece Olivia, and wonderful nephew Omari: I am eternally grateful for the love and brightness you bring into my life. I love you.

To my sister-friend Makai, my brother-friend Kevin, my nephews Tyrone and Kevin, and my darling Justice: you all are my second family. Thank you for always being my biggest cheerleaders. Thank you for all of the wonderful meals and memories we've shared. Thank you for the late-night pep talks. Y'all are my foundation, and we can only go up from here.

To my better half and platonic love of my life, Nicole: thank you for being my muse, my ride-or-die, and my best friend. Thank you for editing previous versions of this draft and being that shoulder to cry on and my copilot on many adventures. I could not imagine twerking in the woods with a better person than you.

Irene, Richie, and Taco. You are my dearest and closest friends and I have loved the memories we've shared over the past five years. Thank you for being all-around fantastic human people. I cannot wait until we can meet up and become our wildest selves again. I love you to pieces.

To my cohort and my doctoral support group at Duquesne: Jillian, Diana, Jesse, Adam, Kelly, John, Josie, Bekah, Rochel, Courtney, Ali, and

Marla, Indy and countless others, I want you to know that if it wasn't for y'all I would have never made it this far. I owe each of you a beer… or at least a fancy mocktail.

Cedric, thank you for being the beautiful human that you are. Thank you for being such a wonderful support system, an impromptu editor, and an all-around amazing friend. I am grateful for your existence and I enjoy our discussions on Black pop divas.

To my loves Brittany and Ryan: thank you for the laughs, the memories, and your friendship. Thank you for those nights of chainsmoking and Yuenglings. Thank you for those morning breakfast sandwiches. Thank you for being my rock through the good and the bad.

To my fur babies Eleanor Rigby and Lucy: you two bring my life joy and happiness…even when you destroy my shit.

Deesha, words cannot express the amount of appreciation I have for you. Thank you for your guidance. Thank you for keeping it 100 with me at all times. Thank you for being you and serving as a constant inspiration. Thank you for throwing a little glitter mixed with Black Girl Magic on me and encouraging me to shine.

Aunt Bert, it hurts that you aren't here to see this go to print, but many of the stories and pictures you shared made this book what it is. I know wherever you are, you are giving them hell and rocking a red lip while you're doing it.

Grandpa, I just wanted to let you know, I'm still letting my little light shine.

Caitlyn Hunter is a freelance writer who focuses on race, gender, and social justice. She is a doctoral student at Duquesne University where she researches African American literature and popular culture. She graduated from Chatham University with a Master's in Fine Arts. She's taught at various universities and was the Emerging Black Writer in Residence at Chatham University. She lives in Pittsburgh, Pennsylvania with her partner and two dogs Eleanor Rigby and Lucy. This is her debut book.

CPSIA information can be obtained
at www.ICGtesting.com
Printed in the USA
LVHW020244231022
731285LV00005B/17